# My Ticket to Tomorrow

## Activities for Exploring the Past, Present, and Future

**Betty Bonham Lies**

**Illustrated by Katy Keck Arnsteen**

*fulcrum kids*
GOLDEN, COLORADO

*To my parents,*
*Bertha Sherwood Bonham*
*and*
*Clarence Samuel Bonham*

Copyright © 1997 Betty Bonham Lies
Illustrations copyright © 1997 Katy Keck Arnsteen

Cover design by Deborah Rich
Interior design by Alyssa Pumphrey

ISBN 1-55591-285-0

Printed in the United States of America
0 9 8 7 6 5 4 3 2 1

Fulcrum Publishing
350 Indiana Street, Suite 350
Golden, Colorado 80401-5093
(800) 992-2908 • (303) 277-1623

# Contents

# Acknowledgments

I would like to thank the Stuart Country Day School classes of 2003, 2004, and 2005 for their helpful critiques of parts of this book. I am indebted to their teachers, Sally Branon, Elena Nickerson, Dottie Woodbury, and Ginny Moore for making time for the critiques. Madelaine Shellaby, Reinald Yoder, Carrol Florkiewicz, Eloise Bruce, Jan Moule, and Earlene Baumunk furnished information used for several topics, and Judith McNally graciously provided the *Earth Day Pledge*. Heartfelt thanks to Suzanne Barchers for her ideas, suggestions, and encouragement.

# Introduction—
# Why a Ticket to Tomorrow?

Because you are alive on Earth, you hold a ticket to an amazing journey: our voyage through time from the past through the present into the future.

Every person on Earth is a time traveler. But you are here at a most unusual place on that journey. Between 11:59 P.M. on December 31, 1999, and 12:01 A.M. on January 1, 2000, lies a moment that comes only once every thousand years. The start of a new millennium!

You've been around for more than one New Year, when we observe the change from one year to the next. That's an important event, and many people want to stay up until midnight so that they will be awake at the exact second the year turns. It's even more exciting to begin a decade, a ten-year period. Many people never in their lives experience a new century. And a millennium is rarest of all.

Ten times one year equals a decade; ten times one decade equals a century; and ten times one century equals a millennium. No wonder people are excited to be alive in a new millennium! Very few people in the history of Earth have ever lived in such a period. It makes us want to explore our own place in time. What has happened to make us the people we are? What is life like right now? What changes will we witness in the future? It's a good moment to look at the past, notice our own lives in the present, and think about what the world will be like for all those who will live during the next thousand years.

## How to Use this Book

This book is designed for you to reflect on your place in Earth's journey through time. It offers you fifty-two topics, each one dealing with a different aspect of life on Earth. In each topic, you can read something about what has happened in the past, record one part of your life right now, and then imagine what the future will be like. There are also ideas for activities you can do to help you explore each topic. You could paste in photographs or newspaper clippings. There are some blank pages where you can add anything else you'd like to keep to remember this year.

The book gives you one topic to think about for each week of a year, but they aren't necessarily meant to be done in order. Maybe something will happen in the world that calls your attention to one of the topics, and you'll want to look at that one. Or maybe you will find an idea that just happens to interest you most during a particular week. Feel free to skip around the book, enjoying each activity as its topic appeals to you.

When you finish, you will have a good record of your place on this planet's voyage from the past into the future, a record that you can add to later when new things happen, or just keep to look back on when you are older. It might even be read by your children and grandchildren.

So take your seat, hang on to your hat, and let's go—on into the future!

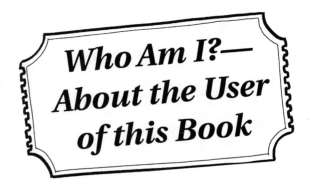

**Who Am I?—
About the User
of this Book**

My name is: _____

This is what I look like (put in a photograph of yourself or draw a picture of yourself):

My birthday is: _____

(month, day, and year)

I live at: _____

_____

I live with: _____

_____

_____

(Name all the people you live with. If you have pets, list them here, too.
Put in photos if you want to.)

My school is: _____

I am in the _____ grade.

I am starting to write in this book on: _____

(date)

Right now some of the things I like to do are:

_____

_____

_____

_____

_____

Some of the things I think I will do in the future are:

_____

_____

_____

_____

_____

My age today is: _____

I finished writing in this book on: _____

(date)

# My Ticket to Tomorrow

# What's in a Name?

STEPHEN CROWN

GEORGE FARMER

MARGARET PEARL

DAISY FIELDS

What does your name mean? Our names are a kind of label. They identify who we are and show that we are individuals. You have a first name, probably a middle name, a last name, and perhaps a nickname.

When the Earth had very few people on it, each one needed just a single name. After a while, though, there were more people who shared the same name. It got harder to know which person you meant when you said a name. So people began to call each other something else too, to avoid confusion. John who was the son of Carl was called "John, Carl's Son," or "John Carlson." John who cut people's hair became "John Barber." John who lived by the hill was "John Hill." John who was unusually small became "John Little." Soon those names became attached to a whole family as their *surname*, or last name.

The Chinese were the first to require people to have family names. That happened ages ago, in 2852 B.C. Chinese family names always come first, not last, and they were all taken from one of the 438 words in a sacred poem. In Europe, most people had only one name until some time between A.D. 900 and 1200. Then, noble families chose a name to pass on to their children, and soon the common people did the same thing.

It's fun to try to figure out where your family name came from. Some are easy. Names like Taylor, Baker, Miller, or Cook obviously meant the work an ancestor did. Other names come from jobs, too, though the words may be old-fashioned now. For example, a Fletcher made arrows; a Cooper made barrels. Names that tell where a person lived are also easy to figure out. Rivers, Field, or Brook are English names of this kind. Ancestors appear in all the names that end with *-son*, or start with *Mac* or *O'*.

In America the name game is sometimes a real challenge. Since most families started in another country, some translation is needed. And immigrants often had their names changed slightly when they got here. For example, "Rockefeller" came from the Dutch "Roggenfelder," meaning someone who lived near a rye field.

Sometimes parents choose their children's first names just because they like the name. Other times they have a special reason for their choice. Many people are named for someone in their family, or someone their family admired. Sometimes family names are given as a first name—so the same name can be either a first or last name. Children may get a name for religious reasons. Biblical names such as John (meaning *gift of God*), Mary (*bitter*), David (*beloved*), and Elizabeth (*oath of God*) are popular. Many names come from Greek or Latin words. Barbara (*stranger*), Philip (*horse lover*), Helen (*light*), Margaret (*pearl*), and Stephen (*crown*) are some of these. Do you think children should choose their own first names?

Many early people thought names had power. They wanted to be known to others only by a nickname. If someone knew your name, he or she would have power over you and could hurt you. What kind of power do you think names have?

## Activities:

1. Make up a private name for yourself that nobody else knows. Write a story about a person with that name.

2. Invent some funny names that make a pun when you say them. Some examples: Althea Later (I'll see you later), Hans Off (hands off), Warren Peace, Justin Time, Rhoda Boat, Harry Legg, Kitty Litter.

3. Think of things that don't have names. Then imagine names for them. For example, what do you call someone who's not really a friend but is more than an acquaintance? *An acquend*. Those little white dots on your fingernails? *Nail freckles*. Add to the list.

**Recording today:**
Write your full name here. What country did your last name come from? Look up the meaning of your first and middle names. Why did your parents choose those names?

**Imagining tomorrow:**
What are your favorite names? What names would you want to give your children?

# Living with Family

Who are the people you call your family? People talk a lot about families, but what does the word really mean?

The dictionary defines "family" in different ways. One definition is scientific and means a group of related animals. In that sense, all human beings are part of the same family. Another definition means a group of people who have the same ancestors. That would include all your blood relatives. When we talk about family life, though, another definition seems to fit best. That is the one that says a family is made up of people who live together or cooperate to raise a child. A family may be united by marriage, commitment, blood, or adoption.

For the first people, families gave a kind of protection. People were safer in a group than alone. The work they had to do to survive could be shared, so that one person didn't have to take care of everything. In most early societies, a family was a large group of people related by blood. This *extended family* included parents and children, grandparents, aunts and uncles, and cousins. Such a family lived and worked together. They could sur-

vive without anyone else's help. Everyone in the family was important. The work of men and women, and children too, was essential for their well-being. Sometimes families would group together to form a larger unit, called a *clan* or *tribe*. Individual families could turn to the tribe for protection or help in time of trouble.

Over time, families changed. In Western countries, the Industrial Revolution caused the biggest difference. Instead of working at home, most men went out to their jobs. They had less time to spend with their families. Sometimes they had to move to be near their jobs, and the large family unit broke up. Now the *nuclear family*—a married couple and their children—was more common. Often, the mother stayed home to raise the children and take care of the household chores.

In recent years, the nature of families has changed again in American society. Greater equality between the sexes means that the "head of the household" does not have to be a man. Both men and women often leave the home to work. They may share responsibility for cooking, shopping, cleaning, and child care. In many families, there is a single parent. In others, adults who are not married raise a child together. Because divorce is more common, many children have more than one family group to identify with. One thing hasn't changed, though. Who we are is still influenced by our family.

## Activities:

1. With paint, crayons, colored pencils, or cut-out paper, create a colorful "family garden." Make a plant for every member of your family. Include both the people you live with and others more distant either in time or place. Who are the trees, bushes, flowers, or even weeds?

2. Start a family scrapbook. Ask family members to contribute things each month to keep a record of the family's life. Include letters, school papers, programs, photographs, anything that's interesting. Any family member can write in something that happened that month.

3. Start a family history book. Get an attractive notebook. When you talk to parents, grandparents, or siblings about some of the topics in this book, write down what they say in your notebook. Everyone will enjoy having your book to look at and learn about the family's past.

4. Make a bulletin board for family news. Anyone in the family can put things on it. Use it for messages, announcements of achievements, artwork, chores, a calendar, grocery list, whatever your family wants.

**Recording today:**
Put in photographs of your family, or draw pictures of them. Don't forget to include your pets!

**Imagining tomorrow:**
What kind of family do you want to live in when you are an adult? Describe or draw it here.

# Make Yourself at Home

Do you know that snug and cozy feeling you get when you lie in bed at night listening to the wind or rain storming outside? You feel so safe! One of the basic needs of human beings is a place to shelter from all kinds of danger. Early people found caves for protection. When they could use tools, they were able to make shelters that suited their needs much better.

All over the world, people build houses to live in. And all over the world, the houses serve the same purpose. They provide safety from the threats of bad weather, animals, and enemies. They also make a comfortable place for people to cook their food, eat, and sleep. But the kinds of houses people build are not always the same. That's because different places on Earth have different dangers, different climates, and different building materials to use. And we create the kind of houses that will suit our way of life.

In hot, dry climates, houses have thick walls and small windows to keep them cool inside. In cold, snowy areas, they are strong and airtight, with heavy roofs, usually slanting so that snow will fall off them. In rainy places, houses have steep roofs, carefully waterproofed, so that rain will run off easily, and no basements to get wet. Sometimes, in very wet places, houses are built off the ground on stilts.

Picture the kinds of houses you've seen in photos of different parts of the world. Then think of the reasons for them. Some people move frequently, like nomads in parts of Asia and the North African deserts. Those people often live in tents. They are portable and quick to set up, and give good shelter against hot winds and dust storms or sandstorms. The Inuit people in the treeless far North build igloos of canvas or animal skins, or of snow. Igloos make tight warm shelters for a bitterly cold climate. In very dry climates, like parts of Africa and the American West, houses of mud or clay are practical and won't dissolve in rain. Japanese homes with tile roofs and light paper screens between the rooms are safer in an earthquake than heavier buildings. People who work on rivers in China and other parts of the world often live on houseboats.

The first settlers in America used whatever building material was at hand, because they had to make shelter quickly. On the wooded East coast, they could put up log cabins fairly fast. When the pioneers reached the plains, they found no trees, and built huts of the thick sod that covered the prairies. As the settlers had more time and money, they made bigger and more permanent houses. Cities grew, giving rise to apartment buildings, where many people could live on many floors under the same roof. But that idea wasn't new. Native Americans in the Southwest had lived that way for centuries!

## Activities:

1. Make a playhouse out of a big cardboard box, like the kind appliances come in. Cut out windows and a door. Decorate it and make furniture out of smaller cardboard boxes.

2. Make a tent house out of card tables and old sheets or blankets. If the sheets are very old, you might be able to decorate them with crayons or paint and cut out windows and doors.

3. Make an "Add-a-Room" miniature house. Find several shoeboxes of about the same size. In each box make a different room. Arrange the boxes so that they make a house you like. You can rearrange rooms to change the style of house. You can even have a garage or a basement. Cut out windows and doors. Decorate the walls, floors, and windows with scraps of paper and fabric. See the next topic for ideas about furnishing the house.

**Recording today:**
What kind of house or building do you live in? Describe it or put a photograph of it here.

**Imagining tomorrow:**
What kind of house would you like to live in when you are grown up? Draw or describe it.

# Take a Seat

*Good night, sleep tight, don't let the bedbugs bite!* Maybe someone has said this to you when you went to bed. You aren't likely to have bedbugs bite you. But during Colonial times in America, people slept on mattresses filled with straw or husks, and bugs were a problem. The mattresses didn't rest on springs, but on ropes stretched both ways across the bed frame. To keep the ropes from sagging, people could turn a screw that tightened them. Then they could "sleep tight." The canopies or curtains hanging over a bed were there for a purpose, too. They kept spiders, mice, or other small creatures from falling out of the roof onto people's faces while they slept.

Before houses had closets, or dressers with sliding drawers, people kept their clothes and other things in chests. Chests are perhaps the oldest kind of furniture. They are easy to make, and can also serve as a trunk for travelers. The idea for cupboards came when people thought of putting chests on top of each other, opening from the front instead of the top.

Chairs were the first furniture meant to hold people, rather than objects. The form of a chair can range from a simple stool to a throne. Its design can be very plain or it can be elaborately carved and decorated. Most important, though, people want a chair to be comfortable to sit in. Upholstered chairs have springs, cushions, and padding to make them softer. Couches or sofas started as a kind of cross between a chair and a bed.

Tables, too, have been around a long time. We know the Egyptians made tables out of stone as long ago as 2700 B.C. An early English word for an eating table was *board*, probably because many tables were just boards laid across wooden supports. In the 1600s, in England, average people couldn't afford a large number of chairs. At the table, or board, most of the family sat on benches. There might be just one chair, for the head of the family to sit in. That person was called the *chairman of the board*. This word for table also explains why a house where people can live and eat their meals is called a *boarding house*.

Most of the furniture we have in our houses today developed from very basic ideas. Beds, stools, and boxes: somewhere to sleep, somewhere comfortable to sit, and something to hold and store our possessions.

## Activities:

1. Make a chest to hold small treasures. Use a sturdy box. A cigar box with a hinged lid is perfect. A shoebox works too. Line the inside with shelf paper, wallpaper, or fabric scraps. Decorate the outside.

2. Make some furniture for your room. Heavy corrugated cardboard is sturdy for small tables. Bricks or cinder blocks with planks laid across them make good bookcases. Pile up pillows for comfortable floor furniture.

3. Find things around the house that you can put together to make miniature furniture: cardboard tubes, corks, matchboxes, small bottles, small boxes, spools, lids from jars or cans, sturdy cardboard, pipe cleaners. Decorate the furniture with scraps of fabric, wallpaper, wrapping paper, tissue paper. Or buy a miniature kit at a hobby or art store and put it together.

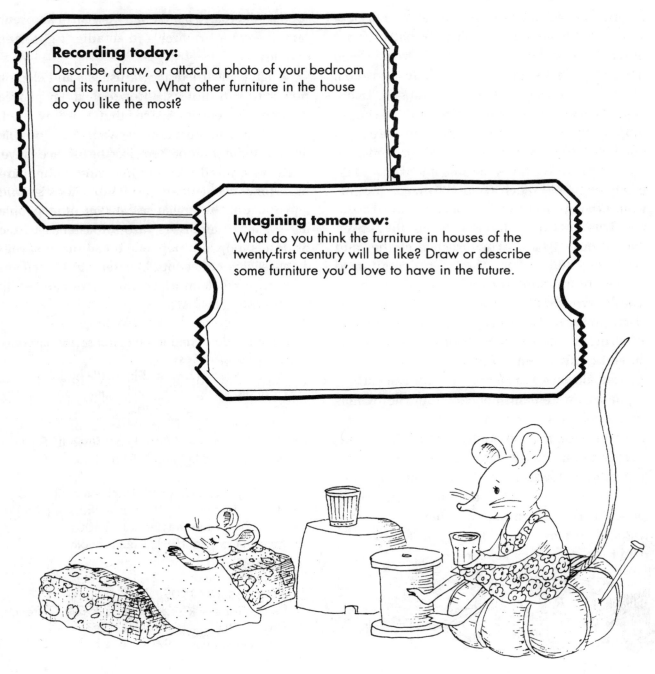

**Recording today:**
Describe, draw, or attach a photo of your bedroom and its furniture. What other furniture in the house do you like the most?

**Imagining tomorrow:**
What do you think the furniture in houses of the twenty-first century will be like? Draw or describe some furniture you'd love to have in the future.

# Appliances—
# Or, What Would You Do Without Your Hair Dryer?

Picture yourself at home in Colonial America, before anyone invented the appliances that make our own houses so comfortable. For heat, you have an open fireplace. In the summer the only way to cool off is to fan yourself. There is no running water, hot *or* cold, and no indoor toilet. After dark, the house may be lit by rush lights, made of the inside of reed plants soaked in grease and used like a candle.

Imagine the amount of time it took just to do the daily chores in such a house! To make clothing, women had to spin the wool or cotton into thread first. Then they wove the cloth. Finally they sewed the clothes by hand. They washed clothes and dishes by scrubbing hard. They swept floors instead of vacuuming, and cooked meals at the open hearth of the fireplace. The only way to keep food from spoiling was to pickle, salt, smoke, or dry it.

Humans, though, tend to look for ways to improve their living conditions. We are always inventing new devices to make life easier. The earliest appliances were hand-operated, not run by machines, so it still took hard work to use them. Even so, it was easier to wash clothes in a tub with a scrub board and hand-cranked wringer than in a stream. Using a carpet sweeper was better than beating rugs by hand. Food cooked better on a wood-burning stove than an open fire, and the stove heated the house better too. An icebox kept

food colder than a pantry or a well. Oil or kerosene lamps gave a brighter and steadier light than candles.

Then we learned how to use gas and electric power to run motors. After that, most people wanted the new appliances that were invented. We're so used to them now, we would have trouble living without some of them, like the furnace, stove, refrigerator, and washing machine. Others are more for convenience or just for fun. Look around and notice all the appliances you and other people use. We have hair dryers, razors, toasters, garbage disposals, popcorn poppers, bread makers, vegetable slicers, coffeepots, blenders, and ice cream makers, just to name a few. Wouldn't our ancestors be astonished by that?

Here are the dates and inventors of some important household appliances:
- flush toilet: first invented in 1589 by John Harington (England), but the kind we use today dates from the late 1800s.
- refrigerator: 1834, gas refrigeration
- sewing machine: 1845, Elias Howe (U.S.)
- gas stove and lighting: 1855, Robert W. Bunsen (Germany)
- washing machine: 1858, Hamilton Smith (U.S.)
- electric light: 1879, Thomas A. Edison (U.S.)
- pump and water heater: late 1800s
- vacuum cleaner: 1901, Hubert Booth (England)
- air-conditioning: 1902
- electric range: 1909
- freezer for quick-frozen foods: 1924, Clarence Birdseye (U.S.)
- microwave oven: 1940s

**Activities:**

1.  With the help of an adult, make a stove to cook on. Cut a door in the front of a large coffee can with tin snips. Cut a smaller door on the back. On a bare flat surface outdoors, turn the can upside down and build a fire inside with twigs. Put a little salad oil on the top of the can. Fry an egg, cook a pancake, make a grilled cheese sandwich, or grill a beef hot dog.

2.  How many appliances, gadgets, or labor-saving devices can you find in your house? List them under these headings: Electric, Battery-operated, Gas-powered, Hand-operated. Are you surprised at the number?

3.  What new appliances have appeared since your parents or grandparents were children? What changes have they seen in heating, lighting, housekeeping devices, and other appliances?

**Recording today:**
What appliances around the house would you hate living without? What do you yourself use most often?

**Imagining tomorrow:**
What new inventions might make living easier or more pleasant for people in the future? Invent some appliances for the twenty-first century and draw or describe them here.

# The Other Family—Pets

Did it ever strike you as funny that different kinds of animals can live together happily? People, dogs, cats, fish, birds, gerbils—all in one house. We and our pets make a special kind of family.

This friendship has been going on for thousands and thousands of years, ever since people began to think that animals could be helpful to them. Probably, the first animals that humans tamed (*domesticated*) were dogs, to help with hunting. People then tamed other animals, like cattle and sheep, for food. Donkeys, horses, and camels were useful to carry things. Cats could protect food supplies from mice and rats. Some kinds of pigeons could carry messages. Bees could help pollinate fruit trees as well as make that good sweet stuff, honey.

Somewhere along the line, people began to become fond of their animals. They just liked the company. Then they started keeping them as pets.

The ancient Egyptians not only kept cats, they worshiped them. They also worshiped baboons, and used hyenas for hunting, the way people today use dogs. Ancient Assyrians kept large mastiffs as hunting dogs. Ancient Romans kept horses and dogs, and sometimes more unusual animals. One emperor, Caracalla, owned a pet lion named Scimitar. His lion ate at the table with Caracalla, and slept at the foot of his bed. The Romans, who loved circuses, taught elephants to perform, and apes to ride dogs and chariots. In the Middle Ages, hunting with tame hawks or falcons was a favorite sport.

Probably today's most common pets are cats and dogs, birds and fish. But we make pets of all sorts of animals. People keep small furry animals like gerbils, hamsters, guinea pigs, and mice. Rabbits are popular, too. Some people have pet snakes. Others keep unusual pets like raccoons, ferrets, monkeys, even alligators. Pets that are common in one part of the world may sound odd to people from another part. Crickets and chipmunks aren't unusual in Japan, kangaroos in Australia, mongooses in India, cormorants on the rivers in China.

People have all sorts of reasons to keep pets. Dogs will guard the house, hunt, or herd other animals. Cats are still useful for catching mice. We can ride horses. Some animals can learn to understand commands their owners give them and to do tricks. But probably the most common reason to have a pet is for companionship and the pleasure we get from having them around.

## Activities:

1. A menagerie is a collection of animals. Make a "menagerie" in your room with drawings or pictures of animals you cut out of magazines.

2. Keep a goldfish. If you make a "balanced aquarium," you don't need fancy equipment, just a goldfish bowl. Be sure that besides your fish, you have some growing plants that will produce oxygen and some snails to clean up the bottom of the bowl. You can get all of these at a pet store, along with directions about feeding the fish.

3. Write a story in which your pet or some other animal is the leading character. Or "interview" your pet about its view of life and about its human family.

4. Make animal puppets by cutting out animal pictures, pasting cardboard backs on them, then pasting them to strips of wood about the size of a ruler. Make up a puppet show with the animals, using a box for the stage.

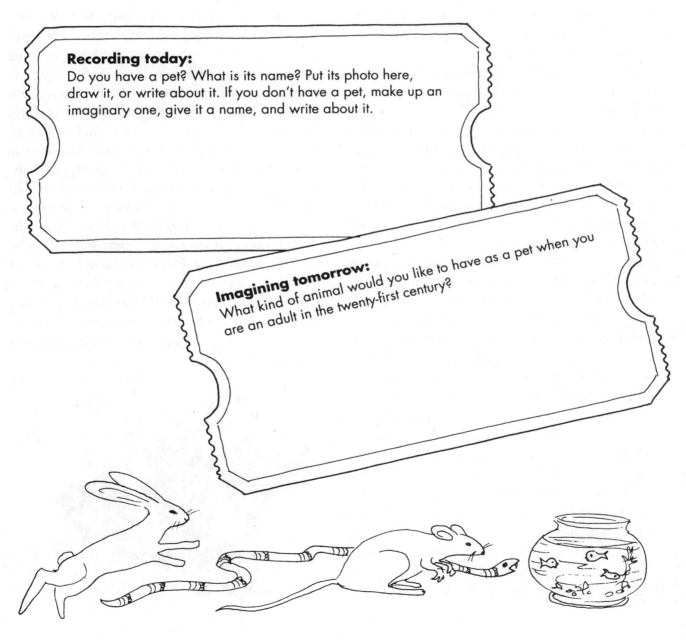

**Recording today:**
Do you have a pet? What is its name? Put its photo here, draw it, or write about it. If you don't have a pet, make up an imaginary one, give it a name, and write about it.

**Imagining tomorrow:**
What kind of animal would you like to have as a pet when you are an adult in the twenty-first century?

# Like a Dream

Every night when you go to sleep, a series of movielike stories starts to run through your head. You may not always remember your dreams, but you always have them.

Sometimes dreams are so vivid they almost seem real. But you find yourself in a strange place, doing strange things. Other people move in and out of the dream, and the places change without any explanation. The pictures or images of a dream are usually what we remember best, although other senses can be involved, too. There may be a lot of sound in a dream, sometimes touch, less often smell or taste. People who have been blind since they were born dream without pictures at all. Most of us dream in color.

Where do they come from, these interesting, sometimes scary, stories? During the night we go through different kinds of sleep. Dreams come when we're in the phase called REM sleep. That stands for "rapid eye movement." We usually have three to five dreams a night, each lasting from ten to thirty minutes. You're most likely to remember a dream if you wake up while you're still in the REM state.

What do dreams mean? To the dreamer, they always seem to have significance. Ancient people believed that dreams came from the gods and had special powers. Four thousand years ago, the Egyptians made a catalog of dream interpretations. The early Greeks, Indians, and Babylonians were firm believers in dreams as omens, signs of the future, advice about curing the sick, or instructions on how to behave. Dream interpretation is important in the Bible. Some cultures believe that your soul leaves your body and lives in a special dream world for a time each night.

The dream theory most common in Western societies comes from Sigmund Freud, who published a book about dreams in 1900. Freud believed that dreams tell us our unconscious wishes. The mind turns the things we don't want to know about ourselves into symbols. If we try, we can interpret those symbols to understand ourselves better. Some more recent theories suggest that during sleep, electric impulses in our brains trigger random pictures. Then, because humans are rational creatures, we weave a story to connect the images.

One thing we do know is that dreams often include things that are on our minds. Recent places or events may appear in dreams, though in strange ways. Sounds that happen around the sleeper are taken into the dream—the alarm clock becomes a buzz saw, thunder becomes an explosion. A lot of people have the same dream over and over again (a *recurring* dream).

We also know that we need to dream to be healthy. If people aren't allowed to dream, they become anxious and sometimes confused. Dreaming is apparently important for good learning. Sometimes, dreams have provided creative solutions to problems that are on people's minds. Several scientists have reported finding the answer to a question during a dream. For many artists, dreams are a rich source of creative images and ideas.

And, yes, it seems that animals dream too.

**Activities:**

1. Use a dream as a source of art. Draw a picture that starts from a dream image. Let a dream or the image from a dream start a story or a poem and just go on adding to it.

2. Imagine your pet's, or another animal's, dream. Write it as a story or a poem.

3. Make your own book of dream interpretations. Make it as silly as you want.

**Recording today:**
When you wake up in the morning, write down as many of your dreams as you can remember. Keep a notebook and pencil alongside your bed so you can do it easily.

**Imagining tomorrow:**
Write a dream you'd like to have. Or, write a nightmare you wouldn't like to have.

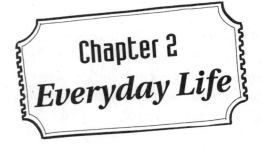

# Chapter 2
## Everyday Life

# In Fashion

When you can decide what clothes to put on in the morning, what outfit do you choose? Why do you like wearing it?

The most obvious reason for clothing is that human skin is rather fragile. We need something to protect us from cold and other dangers. Of course, we have many reasons for the kind of clothes we choose to wear. How we dress often shows things about us: our sex, age, interests, social position, or job. People usually try to dress attractively so they will look their best. But sometimes we are more interested in comfort.

Styles of clothing may seem quite different from time to time and country to country. Yet the kinds of things we wear are really the same. Dresses, pants, coats, capes, shoes, stockings, hats, and gloves are common to all ages and cultures. A particular climate, the activities of a group of people, or their definition of beauty influence clothing styles.

Sometimes a society's idea of morality decides the fashion. In Europe and North America, well into this century, men had to wear pants and women skirts. Anything else would be indecent! Women even wore long skirts to do farm work or work in mines. But in the history of the world, men often wore robes, tunics, or other kinds of skirts. That was the fashion in ancient Egypt, Greece, Rome, the Middle East, and Asia—even in Europe until the 1600s. And women in much of the world wore trousers.

In history, clothing has often indicated a person's wealth or social status. Expensive fabrics and jewels proved that the wearer could afford luxuries. Only people who had servants could wear some elaborate styles that needed lots of ironing or stitching. Sometimes women have had to put up with painful fashions to show that their families were rich—so rich that women didn't need to work. Until the 1940s, aristocratic Chinese bound the feet of little girls. When their feet didn't grow, women couldn't walk far. In many cultures, women are loaded down with heavy gold, silver, or copper jewelry to prove the family's wealth.

We wear clothes of many different materials. Of course, the first clothing was made from animal skins and fur. Very early, though, people learned how to weave cloth from threads of cotton, wool, and linen. The Chinese discovered silk four thousand years ago. Luxurious fabrics such as velvet and satin were favorites during the Renaissance. In the twentieth century, inventors of man-made fibers gave us rayon, nylon, and orlon. Now we can choose clothing made from all these fabrics—even animal skin, or leather, and fur!

Because it's easier today to get clothes and to clean them, we own many more things to wear than people used to. Most people have a different wardrobe for work, school, sports, and dressing up.

## Activities:

1. Make an original "designer" T-shirt. Draw a design with crayons on a plain white T-shirt. Press hard so that the wax gets deep down into the cloth. Put a brown paper bag inside the shirt. Put the T-shirt between two damp cloths and press it with a warm iron. Or make your design with fabric paint.

2. Have a silly fashion show. See who can put together the funniest outfit.

3. Look at pictures of your parents and grandparents when they were children. What styles of clothing did they wear? Do they think it's better to wear the clothes they did or the ones you do?

4. Make a fancy hat out of a white painter's hat. Use colored fabric markers to create a design. Use fabric glue to paste on buttons, sequins, feathers, artificial flowers, or anything else you can think of. If you do this with friends, you can have a fancy hat parade.

**Recording today:**
Do you have different outfits for different activities? What are your favorite clothes? Write about them here.

**Imagining tomorrow:**
What do you think people will wear in the future? Design some clothing you'd like to wear in the twenty-first century.

# Keep It Clean

Let's face it: life on Earth can be a dirty business. People have always had to go to a lot of trouble if they wanted to keep clean.

Cleanliness was very important for many cultures in history. The ancient Romans built public baths as big as swimming pools. There were special rooms for different temperatures of water: the *frigidarium* for cold water, the *tepidarium* for warm water, and the *caldarium* for hot water. Elaborate brick floors carried heat to make steam baths. The Romans even had a special tool, called a *strigil,* to scrape water and oil from their skin. Roman baths were places for people to get together socially as well as to bathe. They could have a massage, do gymnastics, listen to poets, walk in the garden, or read in the library. Often the baths were beautifully decorated with huge columns, statues, and *mosaics* (pictures made from squares of colored glass or stone).

Many societies built public bathhouses because it was so hard to take a bath in a private home. In the Middle Ages, the custom of steam baths spread from Turkey to the Middle East and parts of Europe. The Finnish *sauna* is another kind

of steam bath. Japanese people have always enjoyed public bathhouses. Bathing there requires a particular kind of manners. You wash and rinse thoroughly before you go into the water. The bath itself is a place to relax and socialize. In places where there are natural hot springs or mineral springs, people have often built baths to use for medical reasons.

During much of human history, though, bathing has been an occasional luxury, often just for the rich. We tend to say "Yuck!" when we hear that people used to bathe once a week—sometimes even much less. But just think. To take a bath, they had to pump water, carry it inside, heat it at a fire, and fill the tub. They scrubbed with soap they had made themselves. When they were finished, they had to empty the tub and carry all the water back outside. Their towels and the clothes they wore had to be washed by hand. For country people, laundry meant pounding clothes in a river or stream. City people had to stand in line at a pump and then boil up huge pots of water. If we had to do all that, we might not take a daily bath either—or change our clothes so often.

## Activities:

1. Make a mosaic picture for your room or bathroom. Cut little squares of paper in the colors you want in the picture. Draw the outlines of the picture in dark ink. Then fill in by pasting the paper squares inside the outline. Leave little spaces between the squares.

2. Try washing clothes by hand in a pail of soapy water. Scrub them, then be sure to rinse in pails of clear water until the soap is entirely out. Are you glad you have a washing machine?

3. When you take your bath or shower, try using a blunt plastic ruler as a strigil. Soap up your arms and legs. Then scrape the soap off with the ruler.

**Recording today:**
Do you like to take a bath or a shower? When do you bathe? What is your bathroom like?

**Imagining tomorrow:**
What do you think a bathroom of the twenty-first century will have in it? Describe or draw the bathroom of the future.

# You Are What You Eat

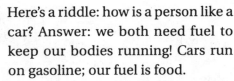

Here's a riddle: how is a person like a car? Answer: we both need fuel to keep our bodies running! Cars run on gasoline; our fuel is food.

You know, of course, that you're an *omnivore*. That means you can eat all kinds of food. The food we eat is called our *diet*. A human being's diet usually includes grains, vegetables, and meat. Some people are vegetarians, and choose not to eat meat. Many vegetarians, though, do eat fish or dairy products, milk, and eggs.

Thousands of years ago, when people discovered fire, they learned how to cook their meat and smoke foods to preserve them. Early humans ate simple meals in groups around the fire. What a huge step from those meals to some elaborate feasts of later years! A banquet for King Louis XIV in the seventeenth century included a first course of many different soups, sausages, and sliced meat; a second course of stews, smoked meat, and salads; a third course of roasted game birds, rabbits, and lamb; a fourth course of small birds; a fifth course of various fish; a sixth course of vegetables, fruits, and sweets; a seventh course of pastries and fresh fruit; and an eighth course of preserves, candies, and sugared almonds. Each course had at least thirty different dishes. That's more than 240 foods!

Needless to say, most people never ate like that. Throughout the world, the basic food of everyone's diet has been some kind of grain, usually rice, oats, wheat, or corn. People made bread from the grain or cooked and ate it along with tiny bits of scarcer, more expensive food. Often, common people ate almost no meat. They couldn't afford to raise livestock, and they couldn't even hunt for wild animals, because the land belonged to the rich.

The first settlers in America couldn't go out to a store to buy their food the way we can now. Their diet depended on what they could get from forests, rivers, the ocean, and their gardens. In winter, people depended on hunting and on food they had preserved by smoking, salting, or pickling it. For most of the year, they didn't have any fresh fruits, vegetables, or salads.

Today, we can choose to eat a variety of foods to keep us healthy. Nutritionists (people who study the importance of good food) say that our diet should start with plenty of whole grains in bread, rice, pasta, and cereal. We should also eat lots of fruits and vegetables every day. The next important food group is protein, found in meat, fish, eggs, and dried peas and beans. We need dairy products—milk, cheese, and yogurt—for calcium, to build strong bones and teeth. The foods we ought to eat the least of are fats and sugar, even though sometimes they're what we like best!

Early explorers learned about potatoes in the Andes Mountains and took them back to Europe in 1565. Potatoes became a major food crop in many countries. By the middle 1800s, poor people in Ireland lived on nothing but potatoes and buttermilk. The average person ate a ton of potatoes a year! The potato blight of 1847 meant starvation for half a million people.

## Activities:

1. With an adult, plan and prepare a well-balanced meal.

2. Tired of peanut butter and jelly? Experiment with new sandwich combinations. Peanut butter and pickle? Cheese and applesauce? See how many healthy food groups you can include in one sandwich. Or invent a new snack by mixing some different healthy foods.

3. For a week, keep a chart of what you eat. Write down everything you put in your mouth. Check it to see how healthy your diet is. Be honest with yourself!

4. What was a typical meal in your grandparents' childhood? Your parents'? Compare with your own diet. Are there big differences?

**Recording today:**
Write down your favorite foods. What was the best meal you've had in the last year?

**Imagining tomorrow:**
Create a menu for a meal of the future. What might a twenty-first century restaurant look like?

# Keeping Fit

Do you like feeling strong and physically fit? Are you happier when you've been active and moving your body? Exercise and food both play a part in physical fitness.

In today's world, many people don't get much natural exercise in their daily lives. Unlike us, our ancestors lived very energetic lives. For early humans, just getting food called for vigorous exercise. Early farmers put in long days of hard physical labor. Work in fields and home both required walking, bending, lifting, and carrying. Those were all good forms of exercise. Laborers at other jobs, too, put out a lot of energy. During the new Industrial Age, in the late 1700s, inventors created many labor-saving machines. Still, the work most people did was physically demanding.

This active lifestyle began to change after World War II. Today, most people can live pretty inactive lives if they want. New tools and machines have made work much easier physically. Better transportation means that people walk less. We can take elevators instead of climbing stairs. We can do house and garden work with machines. Many people sit all day to do their jobs. And TV encourages us to become "couch potatoes," being entertained without any physical effort.

So how can you keep fit in the modern world? The best way is to find some physical activities you enjoy, that make you feel good. If you don't like something, you probably aren't going to stick with it very long. Some kinds of exercise provide *aerobic* fitness. That means the heart, lungs, and muscles become stronger and healthier. Jogging and running, bicycling, swimming, dancing, even very fast walking are aerobic exercises. So are sports like tennis and racquetball, volleyball, and any team sport in which a lot of running is involved.

Today it's also easy to fall into eating habits that keep us from being physically fit. Fast food and packaged snacks are tempting and easy to get. But they contain a lot of fat and sugar—exactly the foods we should eat the least of. People who want to be fit try to cut back on those things, and eat lots of fruits, vegetables, and grains.

The ancient Romans had an expression: *Mens sana in corpore sano*. That means "A healthy mind in a healthy body." They saw the connection between physical fitness and feeling

good emotionally. Health experts today agree that fitness means a longer and healthier life. They also say that people who are physically fit tend to be more relaxed and self-confident. They are better able to face the challenges they meet in daily life.

## Activities:

1. Experiment with different kinds of exercise to find out which ones you enjoy the most. Try bicycling, running, swimming, gymnastics, dancing, or other sports. Read about the best ways to "warm up" and "cool down" before and after exercise to avoid injury.

2. For a week, keep a chart of your physical activity. Write down every day how much exercise you got and what kind it was.

3. Try walking on stilts. Puncture two large (48-oz.) juice cans on two opposite sides close to the top. Drink the juice! Thread about 5 feet of rope through the holes of each can. Stand on the cans, holding the ends of the rope. Tie the rope ends together at waist height. Hold the ropes firmly and walk.

4. Make a backyard fitness trail for yourself and your friends. Set up several fitness stations. Decide on things to do at each station (push-ups, sit-ups, jumping jacks, dumbbells, leg lifts, knee bends, running in place, etc.) You could include playground equipment in the stations. Take turns deciding what will happen at each station, and how people should move to the next station. Should they hop, skip, crawl, run backward? (Bennett, *365 Outdoor Activities*)

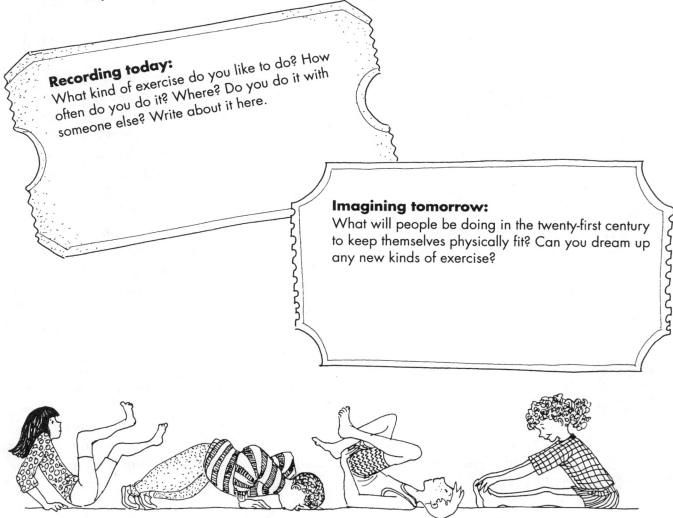

**Recording today:**
What kind of exercise do you like to do? How often do you do it? Where? Do you do it with someone else? Write about it here.

**Imagining tomorrow:**
What will people be doing in the twenty-first century to keep themselves physically fit? Can you dream up any new kinds of exercise?

# The World at Work

Whether you call it your profession, vocation, occupation, job, career, trade, employment, or labor, it comes down to the same thing. Most people have to work in order to live.

The work of the earliest humans was simply finding things to eat. Hunting and gathering food took most of their time and energy. When groups of people started to live in communities, they could divide the work in different ways. Because women had the children, they were less able to go on long hunts. That became men's responsibility. Women prepared the food and cared for the children. Then people learned to make tools, pottery, fabrics, and metal objects. Some were probably better at it than others. They could become specialists and trade the things they made for food.

Ancient civilizations became great when people could work at what they did best. Now, instead of working directly for food, they could do jobs that earned money. Some were farmers and produced the food. Others were soldiers and protected the farmers. Sailors and merchants made trade between groups of people possible. Towns grew along seaports and rivers. Cities needed craftspeople like potters and weavers, and also scribes, law-yers, teachers, and doctors. Builders and engineers were very important to great civilizations like ancient Egypt and Rome. So were artists.

When the first settlers came to America, everyone's work was important for them to survive. Men and women and children all worked together to support the family. Men's work usually included farming, hunting, and making tools. Women's was cooking, spinning, weaving, sewing, making candles and soap. Children helped their parents in whatever way they could.

Until the Industrial Revolution, the home was the center of both labor and family life. Then factories opened to manufacture things, which changed society. Both men and women of the working classes went to work in factories. Even children worked, for as little as 25 cents a day. One slogan said, "The factories need the children and the children need the factories."

In the middle classes, though, men's and women's work was very different. Men went out of the house to work, while women stayed at home to care for the house and children (sounds like those early societies, doesn't it?). Because men earned the money, they became identified as the "head of the family."

When men went to fight in World War II, women took over many of their jobs. But after the war, they were encouraged to go back to house-work. It wasn't until the 1970s that most married women were working outside the home. Larger numbers of women began to enter some tradition-ally male career fields, such as construction work, medicine, law, and business. Today, men and women have much more choice in their work. They are more likely to share responsibility for making money and for taking care of the house and children. And because of the computer, many people are once again working at home.

## Activities:

1. Try baking a loaf of bread.

2. Spend a day at work with one of your parents or an older friend.

3. Try a craft you haven't done before: weaving on a small loom, making bead or shell objects, knitting, assembling plastic models.

4. Make building bricks out of mud. If your soil isn't clay, add one part flour to four parts soil. Add water until it feels like bread dough. Form a rectangle and let it sit until it gets somewhat hard. Then cut it into bricks the size you want with a wet table knife. When the bricks are dry, you can build with them. You can make them stronger by adding straw, hay, or grass to your "dough." (Bennett, *365 Outdoor Activities*)

**Recording today:**
What jobs do your parents do? What work do you do? How do you earn money for things you want to buy? Write about that here.

**Imagining tomorrow:**
What choices of jobs do you think people will have in the twenty-first century? Where will they work? What kind of work do you want to do when you're an adult?

# School Days

What does it take to make a person "well-educated"?

Our first ancestors only needed to know how to survive and get along in their society. Young people learned those things by working beside their elders, and by going through growing-up ceremonies. Nobody even dreamed of schools until writing was invented. Of course, that was as long ago as 3000 B.C.!

In most early civilizations, only boys went to school, and then only talented or wealthy boys. Ancient Greek boys moved from teacher to teacher to learn reading, writing, arithmetic, music, dancing, and gymnastics. Older boys studied *philosophy* (logic, mathematics, morals, and science), *rhetoric* (government, history, and public speaking), and many sports. Boys of ancient Rome studied both Greek and Latin literature and grammar. They went on to higher education if they wanted a career in law or government.

In the Middle Ages, people thought good manners were more important than reading and writing. Upper-class boys and girls *might* study their letters, but they *certainly* learned the skills their society said were important. Girls needed to know about household management and spinning, weaving, and embroidery. Boys studied hunting, hawking, fencing, law, geometry, horsemanship, and magic! The only children who went

to school were boys who were going to become monks. Their subjects were the *seven liberal arts*. These were divided into the *trivium* (grammar, rhetoric, and logic) and the *quadrivium* (arithmetic, geometry, astronomy, and music). Gradually, after the invention of the printing press, schooling became open to a wider number of people.

When America was first settled, the children of ordinary families learned the important life skills at home. Fathers taught boys how to farm, take care of animals, and hunt. Mothers taught girls how to run a household, spin, weave, sew, cook, and preserve food. If their parents could read and write, children learned how to do that, too. Everyone thought it was important for children to learn obedience and religious beliefs.

Then public schools opened. Both girls and boys could go to elementary schools, but secondary schools and colleges were usually available only to boys. Those schools taught Latin grammar, along with mathematics, science, philosophy, geography, and English literature and composition. Girls could be educated at home if their parents thought it was important.

Luckily, though, it wasn't too long before Americans began to believe public education should be open to everyone. Now anyone who wants to be educated can be—if they are willing to work at it!

## Activities:

1. Find out which is the oldest school in your city or county. (Try calling your school district or a librarian.) Does it have a cornerstone with the date on it? Make a rubbing of the cornerstone or any design on it. If your school has a cornerstone, make a rubbing of it.

2. If you could invent the perfect school for you, what would it be like? Write or draw about what the students would study, what it would look like, what a daily schedule would include, and anything else important about the school.

3. Make a list of all the places where you learn things *besides* school. What do you learn from other people, radio, TV, magazines, advertising? Where else do you learn?

4. Think of something you know how to do. Teach it to a friend or to a younger child.

**Recording today:**
What are your favorite subjects in school? What activities that you do in school do you like best? What are you good at? Write about them here.

**Imagining tomorrow:**
What subjects do you think will be important for your children and grandchildren to learn about in the twenty-first century?

# American Schoolhouse

You're probably happy when a school year is over. But how would you feel if you couldn't go to school?

In America's early days, there were no public schools. Children of rich families might have their own tutor to teach them. Others went to private schools, often run by a particular religious group. Then, in 1647, Massachusetts passed a law that said any town with fifty or more families had to open a public elementary school, and towns with one hundred families had to start a secondary school.

The first schoolhouses in America were made of logs or wooden frames and were most often one room with small windows. Sometimes the windows were covered with paper that was greased with lard to let in light. Usually the room had a wood-burning stove in the middle. Students had to help keep the fire going, because in the winter it could get so cold the ink would freeze in the inkwells. The schoolhouse was never locked, in case someone was stranded in the snow and needed shelter. There was no running water, so the bathrooms were outhouses,

one for boys and one for girls. The drinking water for everyone during the school day came from a pail of water with a dipper in it. Students brought their lunch to school in a syrup pail.

A single teacher taught children of all ages. The class was divided into different levels for reading, writing, spelling, and arithmetic. Older or more advanced students would help the others. Because paper was expensive, they practiced their writing on erasable slates. Most students learned to read from McGuffey's *Reader*, which was full of moral and religious stories. A popular teaching method was to have pupils memorize and recite. Some evenings, the town might gather to hear a student recitation or a spelling bee.

The teacher's life was not easy. Often, a young woman right out of high school started teaching in a small school. Some of her students might be her age, or even older. Keeping them in order could be a problem! She lived with the family of one of her students, sometimes taking turns going from one family to another. On her two- or three-mile walk to school, she might encounter coyotes, rattlesnakes, or a blizzard. She was janitor as well as teacher, responsible for cleaning and maintaining the schoolhouse.

Even after schools in the cities and big towns grew larger, many small towns and country areas still had one- or two-room schools. In 1900, there were about two hundred thousand of them across the country. Today, small districts often join together to make very big schools. Now there are only a few hundred one-room schools left in the country.

## Activities:

1. With your school class or some friends, make a play about being in a one-room schoolhouse. Take turns being the teacher. Try recitations or a spelling bee.

2. Find out what kind of school your parents and grandparents went to. Do they have school photographs? Can they describe it? How is it different from your school?

3. Pretend you are a student in a one-room schoolhouse of a hundred years ago, and write a story or diary about some things that happened during the school year.

4. Collect several different kinds of paper: newsprint, construction, typing, homemade, onion skin. Try rubbing shortening on each of them. Which kind becomes translucent, letting light go through?

**Recording today:**
Write about your school. Include its name, address, age, size, and anything else you want to remember. How is it special?

**Imagining tomorrow:**
Draw or write about the kind of school your children or grandchildren might go to in the twenty-first century.

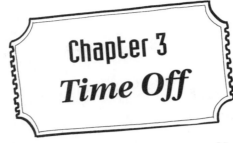

## Chapter 3
## Time Off

# Home Entertainment

*Ho-hum!* No televisions, no radios, no movies, no tape or CD players, no computer games, no telephones. Not even electric lights! How do you keep yourself entertained tonight? If you lived in the days before people had all those things, you wouldn't even miss them. But you would have to find your own amusements.

What would you do on an evening at home in America in the 1800s? Well, first of all, the whole family would most likely gather together in the living room (more often called the library, sitting room, family room, or parlor). Here they would relax together after they had finished their business, homework, and housework. The father would probably read aloud—the nineteenth-century version of radio or TV. Everyone would be eager to hear the latest episode of the new novel, published in weekly installments. Perhaps he would read other articles from the same magazine, or passages from the Bible, or books about travel or science. As he read, the mother might catch up on her mending or sewing. The girls might work on their "samplers" of needlework. The boys might whittle or build card houses.

And how about music? Without radio or CDs, people had to make their own music. Most middle-class homes had a piano or a foot-pumped parlor organ. They might even have a "Pianola" that could play by itself from punched-out metal rolls. Everyone studied singing and music reading at school. Many families loved to gather around the piano and sing together. Or they would listen to a solo from somebody who sang or played an instrument.

Families enjoyed playing games, too. Card games like whist, euchre, casino, or cribbage were popular. Perhaps the adults would play jackstraws with the children, or the whole group would join in a lively game of charades. Someone might start a round of storytelling. Or they would just talk to each other. Conversation was an art in the days before the somewhat antisocial TV came along! At some point in the evening, the family might move to the kitchen to pop corn or make fudge or taffy. In some homes, the evening ended with family prayers.

Of course, for much of human history, few people have had enough leisure time to need entertainment. People who work hard all day are often too tired to stay up and play at night. And before electricity could turn night into day, most people went to bed earlier than we do!

## Activities:

1. Enlist your family's support to try out an evening without electricity. Do everything by candle-light: eat, play games, read, even bathe.

2. Plan an old-fashioned family evening at home. Ask your family to join in reading aloud, playing games, cooking, and/or making music together. Agree that there will be no TV that night. Practice the art of conversation.

3. Make a video or tape recording of your family doing things at home. Include meals, pets, playtime. Be sure everyone gets in on the act.

4. Write a play for everyone in your family to act in. Or get everyone to ad-lib a story you all know. You can tape or videotape it if you want.

Leisure occupations to pass the time in the living room:

      Embroidery
      Making mats of tissue paper
      Crocheting
      Knitting
      Patchwork
      Elegant drawn work
      Phantom leaves
      Making trifles (such as a shaving case
        for brother)
      China painting
      Making feather screens
      Making lace
      Baskets and wall-pockets
      White embroidery
      Wax flowers

      (Taken from Northrup's *Golden
        Manual,* 1891)

**Recording today:**
What is your favorite thing that you and your family do for entertainment at home? Write about it here.

**Imagining tomorrow:**
What kind of "home entertainment center" might you have in your house in the twenty-first century? Draw it or describe an evening at home with your future family.

# Let's Celebrate

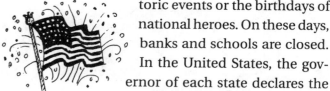

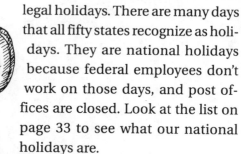

What's your favorite holiday? Why? Is it because you get and give presents? Because it's near your birthday? Because your family does something special on that day? Do you sometimes celebrate days that aren't official holidays? Everyone's answer to those questions would be different. To celebrate something means we think it is important. Some celebrations are joyful; some are solemn.

A holiday is a day when people don't have to go to work or school. Every country has its own national holidays. They usually celebrate historic events or the birthdays of national heroes. On these days, banks and schools are closed. In the United States, the governor of each state declares the legal holidays. There are many days that all fifty states recognize as holidays. They are national holidays because federal employees don't work on those days, and post offices are closed. Look at the list on page 33 to see what our national holidays are.

Abraham Lincoln's birthday (February 12) is a legal holiday in just a little more than half the states.

In the South, several states celebrate the birthday of Jefferson Davis (June 3), and Robert E. Lee (January 19). Many states declare a holiday on January 15, the birthday of Martin Luther King, Jr.

Some special days aren't really holidays, because banks and schools don't close. But we still enjoy times like Valentine's Day (February 14), St. Patrick's Day (March 17), and Halloween (October 31).

Many people observe special religious days. They aren't legal holidays, but they are very important for the people of that religion. The most important Jewish religious holidays are Yom Kippur (Day of Atonement), Rosh Hashanah (New Year), Hanukkah, and Passover. In spring, Christians observe Ash Wednesday, Palm Sunday, Good Friday, and Easter. All Saints Day, Christmas, and Epiphany are winter "feast days." Muslims observe a month-long period called Ramadan. During this month, they fast every day from sunrise to sunset. Buddhists in Japan honor the birthday of Buddha in April by decorating temples with flowers.

Families usually have their own special days for celebration. They might be birthdays of family members, weddings and anniversaries, baptism, confirmation, or a Bar or Bat Mitzvah. What days does your family celebrate?

## Activities:

1. Create your own holiday. With friends, family, classmates, or a club, decide on something you think should be celebrated. Plan the best holiday decorations, activities, games, speeches, food, etc. If you want to invite others, advertise with posters.

2. Write a story or a poem about your favorite holiday.

3. Make a scrapbook of all the holidays you celebrate during the year. Put in photographs or drawings of the day, and other souvenirs like greeting cards, lists of gifts you got or gave, lists of people who were there, programs, scraps of wrapping paper, etc.

4. How did your parents or grandparents use to celebrate holidays? Have traditions changed since they were children?

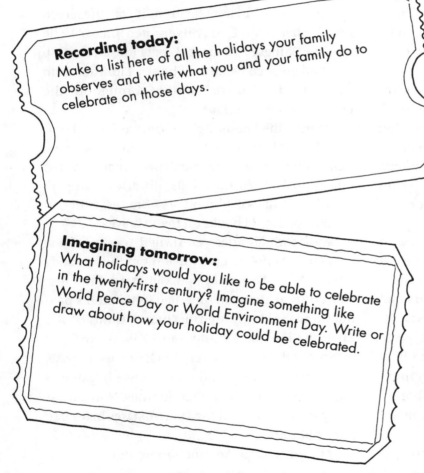

**Recording today:**
Make a list here of all the holidays your family observes and write what you and your family do to celebrate on those days.

**Imagining tomorrow:**
What holidays would you like to be able to celebrate in the twenty-first century? Imagine something like World Peace Day or World Environment Day. Write or draw about how your holiday could be celebrated.

## United States National Holidays

New Year's Day: January 1
Washington's Birthday: February 22, observed on the third Monday in February
Memorial Day: the last Monday in May
Independence Day: July 4
Labor Day: the first Monday in September
Columbus Day: the second Monday in October
Veterans Day: November 11
Thanksgiving Day: the fourth Thursday in November
Christmas Day: December 25

# The World of Books

Do you love that excited feeling you get when you discover something new—a new person, new place, new knowledge? That's the feeling reading can give you. Anything can happen when you open a book!

Most of us don't have enough money or storage space to own all the books we'd like to read. That's why we're lucky to have the library. That name comes from the Latin word *liber*, meaning "book," because libraries started as places to keep book collections. You could think of them as a kind of treasure house. Their treasure is human experience and knowledge.

The books in the first ancient libraries, in Sumeria and Assyria, were clay tablets. There are still thousands of those tablets in existence. Some of them are more than three thousand years old! Ancient Egyptian libraries stored papyrus scrolls, the books of that time. The Alexandrian Library was the most famous. It had a copy of every scroll its librarians had heard of. There were probably more than seven hundred thousand of them. That library disappeared, and nobody knows what happened to its books.

The greatest library of ancient Greece belonged to the philosopher Aristotle. The first public library was the Octavian Library of Rome, started in 37 B.C.

All the Greek and Roman libraries disappeared, too, except for one at Herculaneum. It was preserved by ash when Mount Vesuvius erupted in A.D. 79. The ancient Chinese had great respect for scholarship and had great collections of books. Libraries from China helped spread learning throughout the countries of the Far East.

During the Middle Ages, monasteries and universities had large libraries. All their books were handwritten. After Gutenberg's press made printed books possible in the 1400s, libraries changed. They began to look like today's libraries, with collections of bound books on their shelves.

Most early libraries were owned by private book collectors. Scholars could use them, but nobody else. In 1731, Benjamin Franklin started the first subscription library in America. Its members paid dues, and the library used that money to buy books. Then the members could borrow books without paying for them. Free libraries first opened in 1880, when a man named Andrew Carnegie began giving money to cities for public libraries. Now almost every town and city in the United States has a free public library.

Libraries today do much more than loan out books. They also keep magazines, films, records, tapes, photographs, and computer programs.

Usually, libraries offer lots of programs and exhibits too. Thanks to the computer, most libraries can borrow books from many other places. If your library doesn't have something you want, they can usually get it for you. The library is there to give you as much help as it can with your reading and learning. A free library is the world's greatest bargain. It's worth getting to know!

## Activities:

1. Set a goal of how many books, or pages, you'd like to read in a month. If you can, get an adult to give you a treat when you reach your goal! It's fun to discuss your books with a friend.

2. Start a reading journal. Get a small attractive notebook. Every time you read a book, write down the title and author and the date you finished the book. If you want, you can write a brief comment about the book.

3. Record the books you read by making a "bookworm." Cut a worm's head out of colored paper and pin it on the bulletin board. Every time you read a book, write the title and author on a curved piece of paper and add it to your worm. See how long you can make the body!

4. Go on a library treasure hunt. How many kinds of books can you find? What computer services does your library have? What programs is it going to have in the next month?

**Recording today:**
What library or libraries do you use? What are they like? Write about them here.

**Imagining tomorrow:**
Imagine a library of the twenty-first century. What will it look like? What will it have in it? Describe or draw it here.

# What's Your Hobby?

No matter how busy we are, everybody has some spare time. What do you do with yours? A good way to relax is to do something, not just sit around watching TV. People usually can get really absorbed in one or two special activities. If you do, you have found a hobby.

Lots of people have a hobby of collecting something. Some collect keepsakes, like photographs; or valuable things, like antique furniture. Others look for beautiful things, like works of art; or scientifically interesting things, like butterflies or a list of birds they've seen. Still others collect novelties, like matchbooks or bottle caps. There's probably someone who collects just about anything you can think of! Two of the most popular collections are stamps and coins. A stamp collector is called a *philatelist*, and a coin collector a *numismatist*. Easier to collect than to say!

A different kind of pastime involves physical activity. Many people like to spend their time doing sports. Some favorites are skiing, tennis, golf, swimming, skating, softball, volleyball, or fishing. To keep physically fit, people walk, run, bike, and work out in a gym.

Watching team sports like football, baseball, basketball, soccer, or hockey interests others. Less physical games, like chess or checkers, card games, and board games are fun too. Lots of people love computer games.

Sometimes people like to spend their leisure time together. But hobbies we do by ourselves give pleasure too. Reading takes you away into other worlds where you can live many different lives. Doing puzzles or listening to music are relaxing. Creating a beautiful garden delights many people.

All of the arts make exciting leisure activities. Almost everyone finds that when they do some kind of art project, they completely lose themselves in the joy of creation. Drawing, painting, sculpture, and photography appeal to many people. Others enjoy playing a musical instrument, dancing, or acting in amateur theater. The term "arts and crafts" suggests that they are two separate activities, but sometimes it's hard to see a difference between them. People make beautiful things when they're doing "crafts" like weaving, woodworking, pottery making, jewelry making, or leather working. Building models is another favorite handicraft hobby.

Most people find their best hobbies by experimenting with a lot of different activities. So try out all sorts of things—reading, sports, collections, arts, crafts. Don't worry if you drop some of them after a while. The hobbies of your lifetime—the ones you really want to do—are the ones you go back to time and time again.

## Activities:

1. Start a collection of something that interests you. Consider toys, dolls, marbles, miniatures, picture postcards, programs, stamps, coins, buttons, bottles, leaves, shells, stones.

2. Make a model from a kit you buy at a toy or hobby store.

3. Grow an indoor "garden." Put three toothpicks in the sides of an old sweet potato and set it in a glass of water with the toothpicks resting on the edge. Add enough water just to cover the tip of the potato. Cut carrots or beets two inches down from the top and put them in moist sand. Keep the plants in or near a bright window. Try planting seeds you find in uncooked food, or the eyes of potatoes that have started to sprout. Try lemon or orange seeds (soaked overnight in water), garlic cloves, avocado pits. Water every few days.

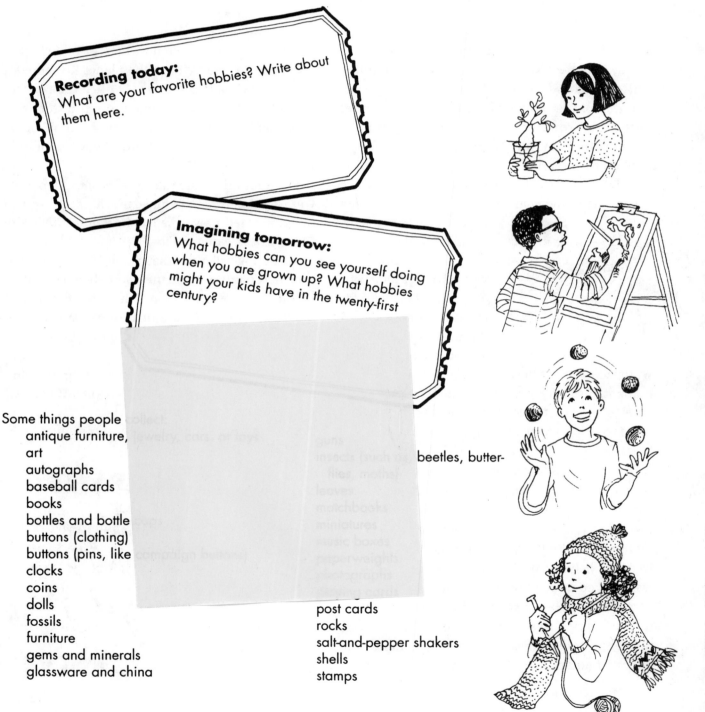

**Recording today:**
What are your favorite hobbies? Write about them here.

**Imagining tomorrow:**
What hobbies can you see yourself doing when you are grown up? What hobbies might your kids have in the twenty-first century?

Some things people collect:

antique furniture, jewelry, cars, or toys
art
autographs
baseball cards
books
bottles and bottle caps
buttons (clothing)
buttons (pins, like campaign buttons)
clocks
coins
dolls
fossils
furniture
gems and minerals
glassware and china

guns
insects (such as beetles, butterflies, moths)
leaves
matchbooks
miniatures
music boxes
paperweights
photographs
playing cards
post cards
rocks
salt-and-pepper shakers
shells
stamps

# Cartoons and Comic Strips

What's the best part of a newspaper? Many people, if they're honest, would say they love the funnies. Cartoons come in lots of forms—comic strips, comic books, animated movies, TV shows, pictures with humorous captions, political cartoons. Whether they're funny or serious, cartoons appeal to almost everyone.

Did you know that the word "cartoon" once meant the drawing an artist made before doing a  work of art? That meaning began to change a long time ago. Around 1500, Leonardo da Vinci, a famous artist and inventor, started using pictures along with words to describe his inventions. He thought that made it easier for people to understand an idea. Later, other artists used words and a series of pictures to tell a story, and modern cartoons were born.

Comic strips first appeared in Sunday newspapers in the 1880s. Some of the favorite early comics were *The Yellow Kid, Happy Hooligan, The Katzenjammer Kids,* and *Little Nemo in Slumberland.* By 1910, most papers in this country were publishing comic strips every day. America was hooked on reading the funnies!

Then people started putting together collections of comic strips in a magazine form they called the comic book. A few appeared in the 1930s, but nobody had yet invented a hero who could grab the attention of the public. Then, in 1938, Superman, the only survivor of the planet Krypton, hit the pages of *Action Comics.* At once the country loved him. From that moment on, the story of a superhero became a popular kind of comic book. Others had funny characters and stories. One favorite was Donald Duck.

At about the time that comics started, people were also beginning to make movie cartoons. The first animated movie, called *Humorous Phases of Funny Faces,* came out in 1906. It was really just a series of single pictures that changed a little bit with each new picture. When they were shown fast, they seemed to move. That's still the basic method of producing animated cartoons. In 1928, Walt Disney made the first talking cartoon movie, *Steamboat Willie,* starring Mickey Mouse.

Animated cartoons have never stopped being popular. In 1937, Disney produced S*now White and the Seven Dwarfs,* the first feature-length cartoon with both color and sound. Today, some of the most popular movies are animated. What are your favorites?

## Activities:

1. Create some funnies with a friend. Each person draws the pictures of a comic strip without words. Put in a lot of action. Exchange strips and write words to go with what's happening in the other person's pictures.

2. Use stamps and stickers to create a comic strip. Draw more pictures around them if you want to add other things to the story.

3. Make a comic strip print. Rub a white candle all over a piece of plain white paper until the paper is waxy. Cut pictures out of colored funnies and lay them face down on the waxy paper. Rub the picture with the bowl of a spoon to transfer the print on to the waxy paper. Put together pictures from different strips to make a funny comic.

4. What story do you know that would make a good animated cartoon? Draw pictures to show what one scene might look like.

**Recording today:**
What are your favorite comic strips, comic books, or animated cartoons? Write them down here. Paste in or draw a picture of your favorite cartoon character.

**Imagining tomorrow:**
Imagine a comic strip you might draw in the twenty-first century. Would it be funny, an action strip, a fantasy, or a family story? What kind of characters would it have? Invent a character, or more than one character, and name them. Draw an episode of your comic strip.

Draw your own comic strip here.

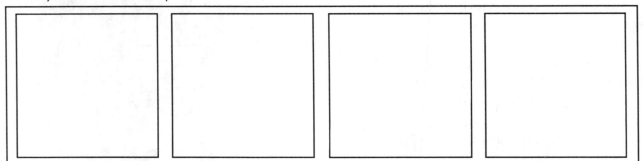

# Be a Sport

What's your sport? Do you play or are you a spectator? Sports events probably started as competitions between early people in the skills they needed for survival. Most games still ask athletes to be good at those things: running, throwing, or jumping. Sometime in the past, someone came up with the idea of throwing around an air-filled bladder. That was the first ball. It changed sports forever. Think of all the games today that use balls of different sizes, shapes and materials!

In the twentieth century, Americans became fascinated by sports. The turn of the century brought a new passion for both playing and watching games. Football was often wild and violent. In 1905, nineteen high school and college players were killed during games! Baseball became a popular sport too. In 1903, a new major league, the American, arose to rival the old National League. That was the year of the first World Series game. In boxing, people cheered on their favorites in the "Battle of the Century" between Jim Jeffries and Jack Johnson, the first famous African-American athlete. Another star of the time was Jim Thorpe, a Native-American football player and Olympics champion.

During the 1920s, sports became more popular than ever. Sports writers raised the interest of people in both games and athletes. Some of the great sports figures were Babe Ruth in baseball, Red Grange in football, Jack Dempsey and Gene Tunney in boxing, Helen Wills and Bill Tilden in tennis, Johnny Weissmuller and Gertrude Ederle in swimming, Bobby Jones in golf, the horse Man O'War in

horse racing. A lot of sports heroes of the twenties went on to star in terrible movies, suggesting that athletics and acting require two very different talents!

Another change in sports came after World War II with the rise of African-American athletes. Jackie Robinson and Satchel Paige were the first in baseball, Marion Motley in football. In the 1960s, professional sports became a big moneymaker. Athletes began to get rich from huge salaries, endorsements of products, and businesses on the side.

People all over the world also love a different kind of sports event: the Olympic games, in which athletes from many countries compete. The Olympics were held in ancient Greece and combined religion and sports. They were open only to men, and women couldn't even attend as spectators! Fortunately, that has changed now. The first modern Olympic games took place in Athens in 1896. Now summer and winter Olympics are held every four years, in different countries. Their aim is to promote peace and friendship among nations. The Olympics are open to athletes from all countries of the world.

## Activities:

1. The Olympic games often have a new sport that wasn't allowed last time. Imagine a funny sport that you'd like to see in the Olympics. Write a letter arguing that the Olympic Committee should adopt your sport. (This can be serious if you think there's really one that should be an Olympic sport but currently isn't.) Be as persuasive as you can.

2. Make a poster advertising your favorite sport, or your funny one.

3. With friends, stage an Olympic balloon event. Blow up a lot of balloons. Some competitions could be: keeping them in the air by blowing or hitting them with hands, a cardboard tube, wooden spoons, or your feet (lying down); shoot baskets with balloons and a paper bag; long-distance balloon toss; balloon balance as you walk across the floor with one on your head. (Bennett, *Cabin Fever*)

4. Become an expert in your favorite sport by finding out all you can about its history and its players. "Interview" one of your favorite players.

**Recording today:**
What sports or games do you like to play? What do you like to watch?

**Imagining tomorrow:**
What new sports might be played in the twenty-first century? Dream up a new kind of game and draw or write about it here. Or write about the sports you'd like to play when you are an adult.

# Anyone for a Game?

"What should we do?" Long summer days to be filled, hours after school—how do you spend that time? In the days before TV and electronic games, children would get together to play games on the playground, in someone's yard, even in the street. The very best times were summer evenings, after dinner, while shadows lengthened into night.

Evening is perfect for *Hide and Seek* or some of its variations. In *Kick the Can*, the hiders try to sneak back to kick the empty tin can that was set up before the game started. Another game, called *Washington Poke* or *Polka Dot Circle*, starts with the group drawing a circle on the back of the person who's IT. One person pokes the back, and IT has to guess who poked. If IT is right, that person becomes IT, while everyone else scatters to hide.

There are lots of different running games. Catching someone else is often the aim of these games. Tag is probably the best known, but there

are many others. *Run Sheep, Run* is a team game, where the "sheep" have to run when their leader says to. In *Red Light, Green Light*, when IT says, "Green light!" everyone (behind ITS back) runs to get to a particular place. When IT says, "Red light!" and turns around, everyone has to stop, and if IT sees anyone moving, that person is "out." For *Red Rover*, two teams face each other in lines, holding hands. When they call out, "Red rover, red rover, send blue over," everyone who's wearing that color has to run across and try to break through the line. *Blind Man's Bluff* is a tag game where IT is blindfolded.

*Crack the Whip* involves a line of children running while holding hands. The first person stops and begins to "crack the whip." The trick if you're at the end of the line is to keep hold and not be thrown off. Human sculpture is the aim of *Statue Maker*. The "sculptor" secretly decides on a shape for the statues. Then the sculptor spins each player around and lets go. They have to freeze in the position they end in. The one who looks most like the shape gets to be the next statue maker.

*Follow the Leader* has many variations. Most people know the trick of *Simon Says*, where you obey the command only if the leader has said "Simon says" first. Another version of that is *Captain, May I?* The Captain tells people how many steps they can take, what size, and in what direction. They can't do it unless they ask, "Captain, May I?" and get the answer, "Yes, you may."

Some games involve making up plots as you go along, and acting them out. Most of those games involve life experiences, like *House* or *School. Cops and Robbers* pits "good guys" against "bad guys." Games of skill like *Hopscotch* and *Jump Rope* have been around for a long time. To be good at them, or at *Jacks, Marbles, Tops,* or *Yo-yos,* takes practice. In many cities, children play versions of team games that don't use a lot of equipment. *Stickball, Stoopball,* and *One O'Cat* are a few.

Children's games were always passed down from one age group to the next. They weren't taught by adults. Now, of course, a lot of children play video or computer games that have been invented by adults. Does anyone play the old games any more?

## Activities:

1.  Find out about some games your parents and grandparents played when they were children, or read about old games. Try them with your friends. See how good you can get at marbles, jacks, or Yo-yos.

2.  Find all the jump rope rhymes you can. Practice jumping to them. Try Double Dutch, with two ropes. Make up new rhymes.

3.  Invent some new games. For example, try drawing or hitting a target blindfolded. What games could you make up that use marbles? A ball? What games could you invent where you have to improvise a plot?

**Recording today:**
What kinds of games do you play with your friends?

**Imagining tomorrow:**
What will your children do for amusement? What kind of games might they play in the twenty-first century? Draw or write about them.

# Toy Story

If you could save one toy from your childhood to give to your own children, what would it be? All through history, children have played with pretty much the same basic kinds of toys.

One of the first toys for babies is a toy animal. Stuffed fuzzy animals seem to appeal to people of every age! Some animal toys are big, like rocking horses, which a child can ride. Others are very small miniatures. A toy that was popular for a long time was Noah's Ark, with two of every kind of animal. Many children have zoo or farm sets with little animals. Animal pull toys, made of wood or tin, and now sometimes plastic, have been around for a long time.

Another toy little children like to play with is blocks. Piling up and watching them fall down seems to be very satisfying. When they get a little older, children build houses and even cities out of blocks of all sizes and shapes.

Dolls have been favorite toys for a long time. They go back to the earliest civilizations. The Metropolitan Museum in New York has a carved wood doll from ancient Egypt that's about four thousand years old! Dolls don't have to be fancy. Children in the past often had dolls made out of corn husks or clothespins, dolls with heads of dried apples or papier-mache, dolls sewn from rags or animal skins. Stylish dolls appeared in the eighteenth century. Those dolls first had heads made of wax. Later, painted porcelain made very lifelike heads, hands, and feet. And dollhouses? Everybody loves them, with their miniature furniture and dolls to live in them.

Girls had dolls; boys had soldiers. Every boy of the nineteenth century had lead or tin soldiers to take into battle. In the twentieth century, girls had Barbie, but boys had G.I. Joe. Toy cars, trucks, trains, airplanes, and other vehicles were once considered boy toys, but of course girls like them too.

In the 1800s, mechanical toys were the rage. These toys, also called *automata*, had parts that made them move. Most of them had mechanisms that wound up like clocks. Then dancers would twirl, acrobats would spin, animals would walk. Another kind of mechanical toy was a bank that made some action happen when you dropped a coin in. Moving toys in the twentieth century more often operate on batteries.

Optical toys are still intriguing. You've probably looked through a kaleidoscope to see beautiful, constantly changing patterns. They are made by chips of colored glass reflecting off mirrors. The stereopticon made pictures look three-dimensional. Other toys gave the impression of moving pictures.

So many toys! Board games, pop-up books, tops, hoops, marbles, jacks, and on and on. Most kinds of toys have been around for ages. The late twentieth century, though, saw a new kind, the *elec-tronic* game: video games and computer games. Do you think they will replace all those other toys in the future?

## Activities:

1. Make an apple puppet head. Peel and core an apple and carve it into a face with a dull knife. Put it in a bowl of salty water for an hour. Take it out and carefully dry it. Put a popsicle stick in the bottom and set it in a weighted-down tall soda bottle. Let it dry and watch the face change. Make clothes for the puppet and give a show.

2. Do you have an idea for a new toy or an improvement on one? Draw it up and write to a toy company to suggest they make it.

3. Visit a museum that has old-fashioned toys and dolls.

4. What toys did your parents and grandparents play with? Did they save any of them?

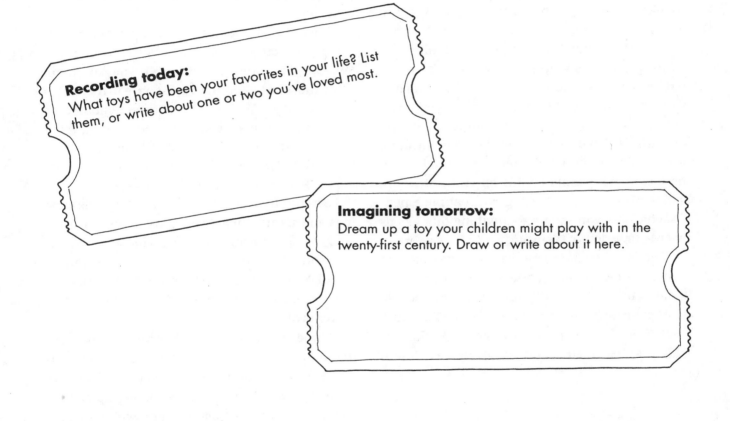

**Recording today:**
What toys have been your favorites in your life? List them, or write about one or two you've loved most.

**Imagining tomorrow:**
Dream up a toy your children might play with in the twenty-first century. Draw or write about it here.

# Now You See It

Are you an artist? Of course! Everyone enjoys some kind of art. Art includes all sorts of things. Music and dance are arts. So are poetry and novels and drama. You could say that every creative skill is an art. Often, though, we use the word just to mean the visual arts: drawing, painting, and sculpture.

People will pick up just about anything and make a picture with it. We draw with sticks on sand, with soft stones on other stone surfaces. Very small children take a crayon or a pencil and draw all over anything that's handy, including books or furniture or the walls. In school, at meetings, or talking on the telephone, people doodle all over notebooks or pads of paper. We love using charcoal, pens, pencils, chalk, crayons, paints—anything that lets us record our vision of the world.

The earliest paintings we've seen are so old that we don't know anything about their creators. Deep in caves in France and Spain, prehistoric people painted beautiful pictures of animals. They often used the shapes of the cave walls to make the animals look real. In other countries, too, we've found

pictures painted and scratched on stone. Some of those paintings were made as far back as fifteen thousand years ago. People have been painting ever since.

We draw and paint for a lot of reasons. Sometimes you want to express how you're feeling, and you can do that in a painting. Or you see something that's so beautiful you just have to try to capture it on paper. You might want to remember some moment, some person or animal, something about life, and the way you felt at that moment. Sometimes you want to make a design or put together colors. Perhaps you just feel creative.

Sculpture is even older. People have made carvings and statues for at least thirty thousand years. Unlike paintings or drawings, which are usually done on a flat surface, sculpture is three-dimensional. You are meant to look at it from many different angles. Mobiles are sculptures that move in currents of air.

Some art is *representational;* the artist is showing something that you can recognize. *Abstract* art is more concerned with form than reality. In between the two extremes—from photographic realism to complete abstraction—lie a wide variety of styles. One of the great things about visual art is that there are so many different subjects and styles and individual interpretations of life. That's why we go to museums to look at the art other people have created. That's also why we create art. It's our way of interpreting the outside world from inside the world that's us.

## Activities:

1. Try a piece of "mixed media" art. Take all sorts of things that people might consider junk. Glue them together into interesting shapes. Paint them, paste on other things like ribbon or yarn, cut-up paper, glitter, buttons, anything. Make something *you* find interesting or attractive.

2. Try out as many different materials as you can to draw or paint with: crayons, pastels, water colors, acrylic paint, charcoal, pens of different kinds, pencils and colored pencils, etc. What do you find most pleasing?

3. Be a sculptor. Carve a statue out of a bar of soap. Make a mobile. Start with a coat hanger and attach some more hangers. Hang some other things from them by string. Watch out for balance!

4. Go to an art museum and look at some paintings and sculpture. Find what pleases you the most. Look at it for a long time, noticing shapes, colors, what it makes you think or feel. Make a sketch or a description in words. See if you can find a postcard of it in the museum gift shop. If you've written down things about it, make a poem from some of the words.

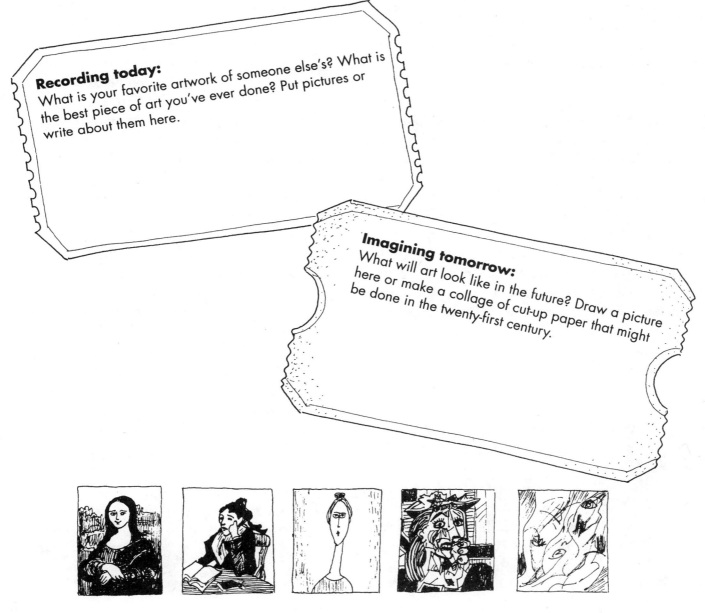

**Recording today:**
What is your favorite artwork of someone else's? What is the best piece of art you've ever done? Put pictures or write about them here.

**Imagining tomorrow:**
What will art look like in the future? Draw a picture here or make a collage of cut-up paper that might be done in the twenty-first century.

# Say Cheese

How would you like to have a magic mirror that could show you things about the world you had never known before? It could tell you about people or about nature. It could show the society you live in. Then it could look inside you to help you understand about yourself. Well, we do have such a mirror. It's called the camera.

Photography was invented in the early 1800s. Since then, people have come to rely on pictures more and more. We keep them as a record of who we are and where we've been. We study pictures of the past to see how people used to live. But photography has done something even bigger. It has made us visual people. Today, we get most of our information about the world through photos. The images they create tell us what is real. We see things in a new way when a photograph points out details we've never noticed. We learn what our society is like by looking at pictures of what we do and what we have. We want things because we've seen pictures of them.

People say, "The camera can't lie." But does a photograph always tell the truth? It certainly captures a real moment of time and a bit of space. Yet it can only show a fragment of that time and space. And when photographers take a picture, they 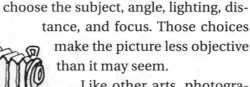 choose the subject, angle, lighting, distance, and focus. Those choices make the picture less objective than it may seem.

Like other arts, photography is creative and intrigues our imagination. A good photograph invents something that we recognize as true, even if it's not just a historical record. A picture that's taken very close up, or shows only part of an object, can be like an abstract painting. You may not know exactly what it is and still enjoy its beauty or its oddness. To create their art, photographers can do all sorts of things when they make pictures. Sometimes they take double exposures or combine negatives for special effects. They may cut pictures apart and rearrange the parts, draw or write or paint on them. Developing negatives in different ways can create different effects in the final photo.

For most of the time photography has been around, the camera was basically the same. It was a box with a small opening that let in light when the shutter opened and closed fast. Light-sensitive film inside recorded an image. To make the photograph, a person developed the film in a darkroom.

The Polaroid camera was the first new way of getting pictures. It let people see a photo right away. Now the computer has really changed the way photography is done. Cameras can send an image right into the computer. Using a computer program, a photographer can change any image. A photograph can even be completely invented by the artist. The computer does it so  well we can't tell what is real and what is made up! Will this change the way people think of photos in the future?

## Activities:

1. Make a scrapbook of pictures you like, cut from magazines. They might be dreams—places you'd like to go or things you'd like to see. Collect pictures of one kind of thing, like animals or interesting people. Or collect images that intrigue you.

2. Take some photographs or magazine pictures and change them. Cut them up and put them together in odd ways; combine different images; draw or paint on them; take parts of them and paste them in patterns on colored paper; paste tissue paper or glitter on them. Use your imagination to create different effects.

3. If there is a camera you can use, experiment with taking pictures that make you see in different ways. Take a whole roll of film of one thing. Do favorite foods, things that are green, things in your yard, or the same thing from different distances or angles. Or shoot over your shoulder, not looking through the viewfinder. That helps you see things in a new way.

4. Make a "time capsule" of photographs of today. Put them away somewhere safe and don't look at them until some specific date in the future, like your eighteenth birthday.

**Recording today:**
Put in your favorites of photographs you have taken. Or put in photos you like of today's world, or photos of your family and friends.

**Imagining tomorrow:**
How might computer photography be used in the future? Could it change school, shopping, people's work, cooking, or other activities?

# A Night at the Movies

Have you ever wanted to draw a picture that looked as if it were moving? Most artists, from the prehistoric cave painters on, have wished they could.

In the late 1800s, lots of people tried to find ways to create the illusion of moving pictures. Thomas Alva Edison succeeded in 1889 with his *kinetoscope*. He took a series of pictures very fast, while something was happening. Then he made the film revolve inside a box. When people peeked through a hole on the side of the box, it looked as if the pictures were actually moving. Edison didn't take this invention very seriously. Other inventors did, though. Soon they found better ways to show pictures that seemed to move. By 1895, people could go into a theater and see moving pictures projected on a screen.

Everyone found this new invention fascinating, but just watching pictures move got a little boring. When they started telling stories, moving pictures became a favorite form of entertainment. The first great hit movie was called *The Great Train Robbery*. After its release, theaters opened in nearly every town in America. The first motion picture theaters were called *nickelodeons*, because it cost a nickel to see a film.

Early movies were silent because sound recording hadn't been invented yet. Some of the dialogue was printed on the screen between scenes as *titles*. In the theater, a musician would play a piano or organ to dramatize what was happening on the screen. During the 1920s, movies became a real art form. Major studios started up in the new American film center, Hollywood. They began to make the kinds of motion pictures we still enjoy: dramas, comedies, westerns, mysteries, action films, and epics. Movie stars became famous.

A startling new film, *The Jazz Singer,* appeared in 1927. For the first time, movies had sound. The "talkies" made movies even more popular all over the world. They became one of the world's favorite ways to spend leisure time. By 1929, 110 million Americans went to the movies every year. Color was the new thing in the 1930s, with films we still love, like *The Wizard of Oz* and *Gone with the Wind*. In the 1940s and '50s, a movie audience would expect to see a newsreel, a cartoon, and a funny or serious "short," in addition to the main feature (or two, in a double feature).

Producers of the 1950s used new techniques like the wide screen of *CinemaScope* to make big, spectacular films. At 3-D movies, the audience wore special spectacles that made things in the picture seem to jump out at them. In *Cinerama*, people felt as if they were actually water skiing or going on a roller coaster. You may have seen some movies in a theater that project a picture all the way around the audience.

## Activities:

1. Watch a silent movie on videotape. With friends, pretend you're in a silent movie and try to act out a skit without actually saying anything out loud.

2. Make a flip book with moving pictures. Think of something you'd like to show happening, like somebody catching a fish. On a small pad of paper, draw a series of pictures. On the figure you want to show moving, change the lines just a little bit from one picture to the next. When you flip fast through the pictures from beginning to end, the figure will appear to move. This is easier than it sounds!

3. If you have a video recorder or movie camera, make your own movie. Write a script and get your friends to act it out. It's fun to do a silent movie with some titles between the scenes.

4. How often did your parents and grandparents go to the movies when they were younger? What were their favorites?

**Recording today:**
What are your favorite movies? Do you have favorite movie stars? Write them down here.

**Imagining tomorrow:**
What new things might movies be able to do in the twenty-first century? Think of all the senses: sight, sound, touch, smell, taste. Where might you watch a movie with your children?

# The Play's the Thing

*Curtain going up!* Another play about to be performed? Or maybe just someone acting out a role in daily life! We do it all the time. Drama seems to be in the bones of human beings.

Plays tell the stories of our lives, the funny and the sad. When you watch a play, you see human conflicts and how the characters resolve those conflicts. It's clearer than real life, because life has all sorts of things going on at the same time. A play can focus on just one situation and leave out everything that isn't related to it. In a play, a character's problems and feelings can be seen more clearly. That gives us a sense of the meaning of life.

Drama is so old that nobody has any idea how it started. Maybe it was part of religion, with priests acting the part of gods. Maybe acting out a hunt made people feel that their hunting would be successful. Maybe speeches at funerals of heroes turned into a play about their lives. Or maybe it was just storytelling around the fire that became more and more dramatic. Whatever got them started, plays have been popular for as long as we know about people.

Plays always have action, character, and a setting or place. Early plays also included music and dancing. In Greek drama, the actors wore masks, and a chorus sang, danced, and chanted, to comment on what was happening on stage. Plays from ancient Greece are still performed, and still have power to move us. As time went on, European plays began to be divided into those with music, usually opera, and "straight" drama, without music. Very old plays that have both music and dance are still being performed in India, China, and Japan.

We put on plays in all sorts of places. Just about anything can become a stage. Ancient dramas usually took place outdoors. In the Middle Ages, plays would be performed on a platform in the middle of a courtyard or town square. Gradually, theater moved indoors.

There are three basic kinds of plays. *Tragedies* deal with the sad parts of life; *comedies* deal with the humorous; and *melodramas* usually have a villain who wants to hurt other characters, while the audience sympathizes with the victims. But all kinds of different things can be done with these forms. They don't even have to be performed by human actors. Puppet theaters are popular in many societies. In Japan and Indonesia, puppets are one of the oldest forms of drama. English children love to watch Punch and Judy at little puppet theaters in the park.

One of the nicest things about drama is that it is so natural. Children can put on their own plays, either with puppets or acting. It's fun to write or improvise scripts, make a theater and costumes, and—*let's have a show!*

## Activities:

1. Drama always has characters, a setting, a conflict, and a way to resolve the conflict. Have everyone in a group write out several lines that could end a play, like "I knew it was you all the time!" or "That isn't what I ever wanted." Draw a line out of a hat and improvise a play that ends with that line.

2. This improvisation is called *Park Bench* or *Hot Seat*. Set up two chairs. One person sits in a chair, waiting. A second person decides who the two characters are, but doesn't tell the first. When the second person starts talking, the first has to catch on to who both characters are, and keep the dialog going. If there are other people around, they can join in at any time.

3. Try being a mime. Without words, act out something, like walking a huge dog, planting a flower and watching it grow, or doing some other action. Focus on action, but remember that the character is important, too. How does the character feel about what's happening?

4. Read a book aloud to a young child. Give a dramatic reading, with different voices for different characters.

**Recording today:**
Have you done any acting? What is your favorite play that you've seen? Write about your experience with drama.

**Imagining tomorrow:**
Where might plays be performed in the future? Will we go to them live or only watch from our houses? Imagine twenty-first-century drama.

# The Sound of Music

*I got rhythm, I got music ... Who could ask for anything more?*

Every society makes music. It satisfies something deep inside us. Music can express all of our emotions and give us a sense of beauty. In early societies, music was an expression of religious feeling. Most religions in the world still include music in their services.

Perhaps people first created music by beating out a rhythm while they sang. Drums were probably the earliest musical instruments. Later, people learned how to make sounds by plucking a string or blowing against a reed. Blowing through a hollow stick made a different kind of sound. So did blowing into a shell. Most of today's musical instruments grew out of those discoveries. The newest instruments are electronic. Their sound can be made louder, or changed, by electricity. The human voice is still one of the most important of instruments. It's one everyone can use to make music.

*Classical* music is music that people have enjoyed over a long period of time. *Popular* music tends to be around for a much shorter time. Songs become very popular, then newer songs come along to take their place. Styles of popular music change pretty fast, too. The twentieth century first heard *ragtime,* then *swing* and *bebop.* Suddenly, in the 1950s, popular music got a whole new sound. It was called *Rock and Roll. Jazz* and *blues* started with African-American music in the southern United States. *Country, folk,* and *gospel* music are some other kinds people enjoy.

Music is one of the few arts that people can be very good at when they are really young. Not many important writers or painters became well known when they were under twenty. But the list of young musicians is long. Elvis Presley was a teenager when he became the first important rock music soloist. The Beatles, who helped change popular music, started when they were about fifteen. Many classical musicians have been child prodigies, especially on the piano and violin. Some of them were giving concerts before they were ten. And, of course, Wolfgang Amadeus Mozart, who lived in the 1700s, wrote music at the age of seven that is still being played today!

Music used to be hard to come by. People had to get together to make music and listen to it. Today, wherever you go there seems to be music in the air. You hear it in homes, stores, businesses, cars, elevators, even when you're waiting on the telephone.

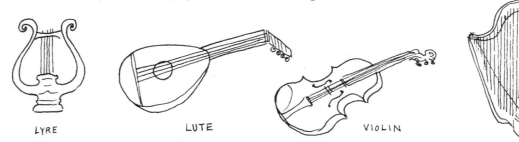

LYRE  LUTE  VIOLIN  HARP

**Activities:**

1. Make your own "orchestra." Here are some instruments you can make. Put dried peas or paper clips in covered plastic containers or oatmeal boxes to shake. Thread metal bottle caps on a string fastened at both ends to a thick piece of wood. Cover two small blocks of wood with sandpaper to rub together. Stretch rubber bands of different lengths between nails on a board and pluck them. Make a water glass xylophone by filling water glasses to different levels to get different notes. Play a tune by tapping the glasses lightly with a spoon. Make a pin piano by hammering eight pins to different depths in a block of soft wood, like pine. Pluck with another pin to get the note. Wrap tissue paper around a comb and hum against the paper.

2. Do another kind of art while you are listening to music. Draw what the music makes you feel, write a story, dance to the music, just write down the daydreams that come. It's most interesting to do this with classical music or jazz that doesn't have words.

3. Write the words for a song. You can use a tune you know and write new words, or add extra verses to a song you know. If you're really feeling musical, write the tune, too.

4. Make your own program of "hit songs." Tape or video yourself, friends, or family singing favorite songs.

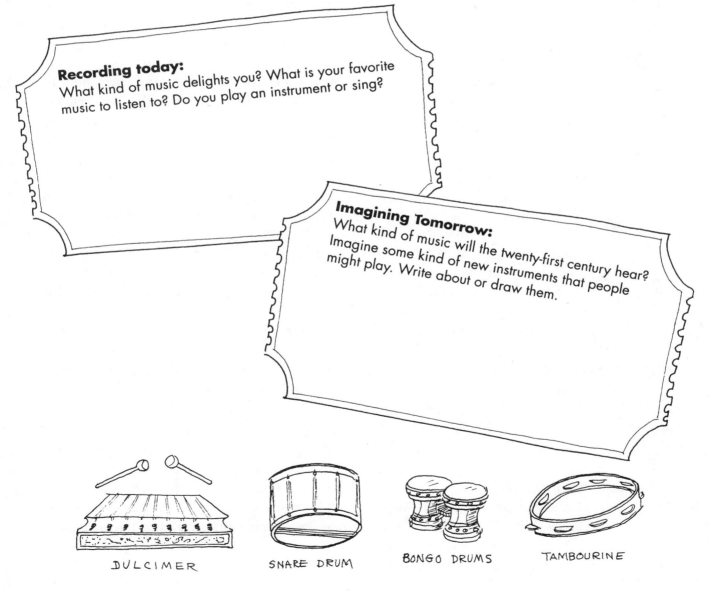

**Recording today:**
What kind of music delights you? What is your favorite music to listen to? Do you play an instrument or sing?

**Imagining Tomorrow:**
What kind of music will the twenty-first century hear? Imagine some kind of new instruments that people might play. Write about or draw them.

DULCIMER          SNARE DRUM          BONGO DRUMS          TAMBOURINE

# Shall We Dance?

Have you ever watched a little baby bounce when music is playing? From children to grandparents, everybody dances. It's one way we express our feelings and use our energy. Ballet, tap, folk, modern, jazz, or ballroom—it seems people just can't stop moving their feet and bodies to a rhythm.

Dance is the oldest kind of art. In ancient civilizations, people danced to celebrate important moments in life, like birth and growing up, marriage, or battles. They danced during rituals of religion and medicine, in ceremonies to bring rain or drive away evil spirits. Music and drama both grew out of dance.

Every country in the world has its own style of folk dancing. Ordinary people did these dances for fun, often at times of celebration. In the Middle Ages, rich and powerful people took up dancing, too. Soon the dances became more elaborate, and people had to be taught how to do them. You may have heard the names of some early social dances, like the *minuet* or the *gavotte*. If you have ever done the Virginia reel or a square dance, you are following the same dance steps that people did in the 1600s!

The biggest change in social dancing (also called *ballroom danc-*ing) came when the *waltz* appeared, just before 1800. Some thought it was shocking. Instead of dancing in groups, people actually swung freely around the dance floor in couples! Other whirling dances soon became popular, too. Some that people still like are the *schottische*, the *polka*, and the *mazurka*.

During the twentieth century, someone invented a new kind of popular dance every decade. The *turkey trot* and *one-step* of the early years of the century led to the 1920s *fox trot, shimmy,* and *Charleston*. In the '30s and '40s, people danced the *jitterbug* to swing music. The '50s *lindy hop* gave way to the '60s *twist,* the first dance based on rock music. The '70s originated *disco dancing*. Other new styles since then have included *break dancing* and *moshing*.

In ballroom dancing, everyone participates. Another kind of dance is performed by experts, for people to watch. Around 1700, *ballet* developed as both entertainment and art. Ballet is a graceful kind of dance that is also very athletic. Dancers leap and spin and move their bodies in beautiful ways. It takes years of training for a dancer to learn ballet movements and be able to do the gravity-defying steps.

A dancer named Isadora Duncan began *modern dance* in the early 1900s. It uses freer, more natural movements than those of ballet. Some later dances move to the rhythms of jazz music. In *tap dancing* the dancers actually become part of the music when they click the cleats on the bottom of their shoes. Popular musical shows today include elements from all kinds of dancing: folk, ballet, modern dance, jazz, and tap.

**Activities:**

1.  In many countries, people still learn the old dances and perform them in national costumes. Find out about the folk dances and costumes of a country your ancestors came from.

2.  Learn some kind of dancing. Ask someone to show you break dancing or jazz dancing. Ask older people to teach you some dances that were popular when they were young. Or learn a folk dance or a square dance.

3.  Make up a dance to celebrate some moment or express an emotion you feel. Choose music and do a dance that goes with it. Move in any way you want. If you feel like it, dress up to match the dance.

4.  Go to see a ballet or some other kind of dance.

**Recording today:**
What kind of dancing do you like to do? Write about it here.

**Imagining tomorrow:**
Imagine the kind of dancing you or your children might do in the future. Make up a dance for the twenty-first century and draw or describe it.

# Slanguage

Would you like it if someone said you were *the cat's pajamas? The bee's knees? Out of this world? Real George? Groovy? Gone?* You would if you know that those are all old slang expressions that mean "wonderful."

Slang is a kind of informal language that uses colorful, imaginative words and phrases. Most of us speak it at some time every day. Slang expressions often start as words used by people in one particular group, then become popular among a larger number of people.

Different time periods invent different slang. In the eighteenth century, if you felt *blue-deviled,* everyone would know that you were depressed or upset. A hundred years later, if you felt that way, you might have said you were *conbobberated.* The 1920s gave us such *jazzy* phrases as *baloney, bunk,* and *horsefeathers,* all meaning "nonsense." During the 1950s, the *hip* world of music brought many new expressions. In one '50s joke, a musician asks a waitress for a piece of pie. "I'm sorry," she says, "the pie is gone." The musician is delighted. "Man, dig that crazy pie! I'll take *two* pieces." (If you don't get the joke, look back at the first paragraph of this chapter.)

All language changes as time goes on. Slang, though, changes faster than the kind of language people write. Most slang words go out of style pretty fast. Nobody today would say you should *tell it to the marines,* or call stylish men or women *sheik*s or *flappers.*

Some slang turns into everyday English. George Washington would have called the word *hoax* slang, but it had become part of the language fifty years later. *Hairdo,* a slang word of the 1920s, was common within twenty years. Examples of one-time slang that we now think of as normal expressions are *ghost writer, cowboy, phone, okay, double cross, gas,* or *cold feet.* Other words, though, have been considered slang for a long time, and still have not been accepted into formal language. Some of them are *beat it* (invented by Shakespeare), *lousy, swell, scram,* or *in the doghouse.*

Well, I'm going to go *do my thing. See you later, alligator. Twenty-three skiddoo!*

## Activities:

1. Start a collection of old slang expressions. Ask people who are older than you what slang they used to use. How many different slang words can you find that mean the same thing?

2. Make a "dictionary" of all the slang expressions you and your friends know and use right now. Can you define them all?

3. Write a play in which people talk to each other mostly in slang, or write a poem that uses a lot of slang expressions.

Match the slang words with the activity or group they came from:

1. ham, wet blanket                  a. sailors
2. hit, racket, scam                  b. trains
3. rat race, blow your top,
   cool                               c. sports
4. stand by, disc jockey, zilch   d. acting
5. brain storm, bull session      e. criminals
6. bail out, flying blind            f. radio
7. caboose, sidetrack               g. aviation
8. above board, overboard,
   keel over                          h. students
9. strike out, make a hit           i. music

[Answers: 1-d; 2-e; 3-i; 4-f; 5-h; 6-g; 7-b; 8-a; 9-c]

**Remembering today:**
What words do your parents say that sound old-fashioned to you? What words do you use that they don't understand?

**Imagining tomorrow:**
Dream up some slang expressions for the twenty-first century. What words might your kids have to explain to you?

GROOVY
HIP
SWELL
AWESOME

# Everybody's Doing It—Fads

What do you feed your rock? If that question sounds silly, you might like to know that many people in the 1970s thought their lives weren't complete without a pet rock.

There's no explaining why something suddenly becomes *the* thing to do. But every so often, an activity or an idea becomes so popular that it's like a craze. It seems everyone wants to do it, own it, wear it, or eat it. Then you know it is a fad.

Two decades of the twentieth century, the 1920s and 1950s, are especially famous for fads that swept America. In the '20s, people entered endurance contests of all kinds. Some did nonstop marathon dancing, competing for prizes. Those contests went on for a week or longer. A dance marathon in Chicago lasted 119 days. That's seventeen weeks—more than four months! Marathon running races were popular, too. One went 3,400 miles from Los Angeles to New York. A man called "Shipwreck" Kelly started a fad for sitting on a flagpole for days at a time. People tried to win fame by breaking records for eating peas, kissing, talking, even bobbing up and down in the water. Many people were crazy about games, especially crossword puzzles and the Chinese game Mah-Jongg.

It was probably that new invention, radio, that spread fads across the country so fast in the 1920s. Television did the same thing in the 1950s. For a while, '50s kids just had to have a coonskin cap like Davy Crockett's on the popular TV show. Thirty million people bought Hula-Hoops and spent hours working on their hip-whirling techniques. On college campuses, students crammed into telephone booths or tiny cars to see how many people could scrunch into small spaces. The '50s fascination with the mysteries of space also started fads. All over America, people reported seeing flying saucers or other strange UFOs (Unidentified Flying Objects).

Fashions often become fads. Take hair styles, for instance. In the '20s, girls shocked their parents by cutting their long hair short in a *bob*. Women in the '30s got tight permanent waves called a *marcel*. The *upsweep*, hair pulled up on the head, was a fad in the '40s. Long hair in a *ponytail*, or very short curly hair in a *poodle cut*, marked the '50s. The '60s saw "big hair" in *bouffant*, *beehive*, and *afro* styles. In the '70s, girls ironed their long hair to make it straight. Boys' hair styles change too. Fads of the '50s included the very short *crew cut* and then the *duck tail*. Long hair and sideburns for men were brand-new in the '60s and '70s. Or you might think so until you look at pictures of men in the nineteenth century!

Most fads come and go very fast. The latest style of one moment can seem old-fashioned and boring the next. Sometimes, though, fads come back. The Yo-yo, for example, has been popular over and over again. And people still try to win a few minutes of fame by becoming world champion at something, however silly that something might be.

## Activities:

1. Try out a Yo-yo or a Hula-Hoop. (You can buy them at a toy store.)

2. Create a play or a puppet show or make a home video about someone trying to teach a pet rock tricks. Or dramatize some other silly fad.

3. What funny fads do your parents and grandparents remember from when they were younger?

4. Find something crazy to make a pet of. Can you get anyone else to want one too?

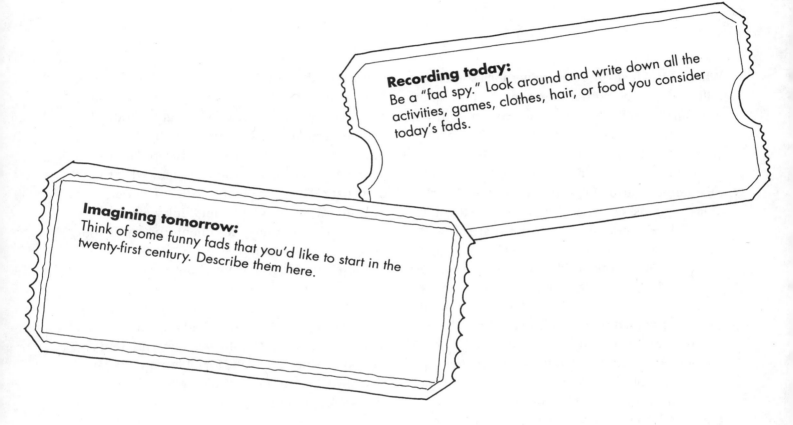

**Recording today:**
Be a "fad spy." Look around and write down all the activities, games, clothes, hair, or food you consider today's fads.

**Imagining tomorrow:**
Think of some funny fads that you'd like to start in the twenty-first century. Describe them here.

# Mind Your Manners

When is the first time you remember somebody telling you to do something because it is "good manners"? From the time you were very little, people taught you how to behave politely. Of course, the definition of polite manners changes from society to society and from time to time. Rules for manners, also called *etiquette*, can cover all areas of people's behavior when they are together.

Table manners are often the first rules you learn. Proper eating behavior has changed a lot over the years. In the Middle Ages, people washed their hands at the table, probably to prove to others that they were clean. That was important, because everyone dipped into the dishes with their hands. Sometimes two people shared a plate. An etiquette book from 1530 told people not to be the first ones to put their hands in a dish. It also suggested that they shouldn't lick their fingers or wipe them on clothes. Instead, it would be more decent to use the tablecloth! But there was a limit. A book from George Washington's time warned people: "Cleanse not your teeth with the Table Cloth."

A description of suppers given by the French King Louis XIV shows the king throwing "little rolls of bread" at the ladies, who were allowed to throw them back. This is probably the first recorded food fight! Today people would not think you were very polite if you threw food at someone or wiped your fingers on the tablecloth.

Rules for etiquette sometimes depend on the invention of a new tool. Forks were introduced in the 1600s. That meant that people didn't have to use their fingers. When they had napkins to clean their hands, the tablecloth was safe. Different societies have their own rules for table manners. Japanese and Chinese children have to learn how to use chopsticks properly.

Sometimes the reason for a kind of behavior changes, even though the behavior continues to be correct. People may have started the custom of shaking hands to show each other that they were not carrying a weapon. Now, a good firm handshake when people meet doesn't just mean friendliness. It also shows self-confidence and respect for the other person. Perhaps in the future, people won't shake hands at all because it spreads germs!

How do we know what is proper? By watching what polite people do, or asking for advice. Many people read etiquette books, which tell the current rules for good manners. Good manners are probably important for two reasons. They help people be together without disgusting each other, and for you, it is helpful to know what your society expects as proper behavior. You feel more comfortable with other people when you know how to act.

## Activities:

1. Look at some current etiquette books in your library. Are you surprised by any of the rules for good manners? What do you think are the most important rules?

2. Invent some funny rules for behavior. With a friend, invent some new kinds of handshakes.

3. Try eating a meal with chopsticks. Try eating a meal with your fingers.

4. What did your grandparents and parents learn about good manners when they were children? Has anything changed?

**Recording today:**
What rules for manners have you learned? Do any of them seem silly to you? Write about them here.

**Imagining tomorrow:**
What will be considered polite in the future? Write down some rules of etiquette for the twenty-first century.

# Heroes and Heroines

Is there somebody you really admire? Somebody you want to be like? If so, that person is probably your heroine or hero.

There are really two kinds of heroes and heroines. One kind lives in the legends and myths of a society. Heroes of this type are usually men who are good at fighting and go around looking for adventure. The ancient Greek hero Odysseus is typical. He spent ten years trying to get home from the Trojan War. During this time he had amazing adventures and solved all sorts of problems with his clever mind. Hercules, another Greek hero, was a man of unbelievable courage and strength. He had to perform twelve "labors." They were impossible to do, but of course Hercules could do them! The old English hero, Beowulf, was as strong as thirty men. He fought the horrible man-eating monster Grendel with one hand. Mythical heroes were usually fighters, and there aren't many women among them. Sometimes women were heroines of stories because they tried to change something that was wrong. The Greek heroine Antigone was a girl who was willing to die for her idea of justice.

Heroines and heroes of legends are always very strong and fight on the side of good against evil. They often have supernatural powers of some sort. The superheroes of comic strips and cartoons are like that. Superman can fly, and he has x-ray vision and bulging muscles. She-Ra, Batman, Spiderman, Teenage Mutant Ninja Turtles, and Wonder Woman are some other examples. They always defeat the bad guys with their special powers. In spite of their power, most superheroes and heroines act like regular people in their everyday life. They never show off.

The other kind of hero or heroine is a real person whom we admire. We look up to great women and men who have tried to improve the lives of others. One such hero is Dr. Martin Luther King, Jr., who led the 1960s struggle for equal rights for all people. Another is Mother Teresa. She helps the sick and poor in India and other countries. Some people find their heroines and heroes in famous athletes, musicians, or actors.

Heroes and heroines can be people you know. Your mother or father might be one for you. So might a brother or sister, or an older friend or relative you admire. Ordinary people sometimes do actions that we call heroic. They might risk their lives to save someone else. But less dangerous things can also make a person heroic. Everybody has the possibility of being some kind of hero or heroine. One way is doing a kind act to help another person. Standing up for what you believe in is a heroic action. So is working to help make the world a better place. What kind of heroine or hero would you like to be to someone younger than you?

## Activities:

1. Invent a superhero or superheroine with some kind of amazing powers. Make up a story about the character. You could write a story or a skit, give a puppet show, or draw a cartoon about the character.

2. Ask your parents, grandparents, or an older friend about the heroines and heroes of their childhood. What legendary ones did they like? Who were their real-life ones?

3. Read about some of the heroes and heroines of mythology. Your librarian can help you find the books. Draw a picture of one of them doing a heroic deed.

4. If you were going to be someone's heroine or hero, what qualities would you want to be admired for? Draw or write a story about yourself as a hero or heroine.

**Recording today:**
Who are your heroes or heroines? Why do you look up to them? Write about them here.

**Imagining tomorrow:**
What kind of person do you think will be admired in the twenty-first century? Write about or draw a heroine or hero of the future. Or imagine a superhero of the next millennium and draw or describe him or her. What super powers would the character have?

# In Sickness and in Health

You know that feeling when you've been sick and get well again? Then you know what it's like to be healthy. The human body is pretty strong, but it can also get sick or hurt. That's why the art of healing started early in human history.

At the beginning, people thought diseases were caused by evil spirits. Priests, rather than doctors, treated them. But those early people weren't dumb. They learned that many plants can help heal the sick. Egyptian and Hebrew doctors found all sorts of ways to treat injuries and prevent disease. The Chinese developed acupuncture, which people still use. Ancient Indian doctors were skilled at surgery. Greek and Roman doctors made medicine a science.

Today we often take for granted many of the most important medical discoveries. It's hard even to imagine how many lives they have saved. In 1676, Anton von Leeuwenhoek discovered the tiny organisms called germs or bacteria. Vaccination was first done in 1796. Now we have all kinds of inoculation to make people immune to certain diseases. In the mid-1800s, many scientists tried to find a safe anesthetic that would put people to sleep during an operation. Ether was the first practical one. Suddenly, doctors could perform operations that they couldn't have done before. Louis Pasteur, in the late 1800s, proved that bacteria cause disease, and that killing them can stop the spread of many diseases. Then Joseph Lister realized that dirty hospitals and operating rooms were causing patients to die. He introduced ways to make surgery sterile. Now research into human genes promises to find cures and prevention for all sorts of diseases.

Health problems change from century to century. It's odd, but as we find ways to prevent or cure one disease, another one seems to crop up. Leprosy was a major terror from 500 to the 1200s in Europe. The bubonic plague, called the Black Death, killed about a quarter of Europe's population in the mid-1300s, and kept coming back until the 1600s. Smallpox killed and scarred people terribly until Edward Jenner found a vaccine against it. People in the 1800s feared tuberculosis, also called consumption. It caused early death for people around the world. So did outbreaks of influenza, especially in the early 1900s. Antibiotics, discovered after World War II, proved to cure tuberculosis and pneumonia. Polio was a scary disease until a vaccine was invented in the 1950s. A new disease of the late twentieth century is AIDS.

The good news is that constant research and discoveries in medicine have taught us more and more about what causes diseases. That helps both to prevent and cure them. Maybe the time will come when people won't get sick at all!

**Activities:**

1. When a friend or sibling is sick, think of a way to help them feel better. Make a book of things to do: puzzles, games, paper dolls, riddles, jokes, any activity that will amuse them.

2. Invent a silly new disease, like "coronosis of the knee." Make a poster advertising how it can be prevented or cured. For example: "25 M & M's every day after lunch."

3. Have you had all your inoculations? How about your pet? What do you do to keep yourself healthy and physically fit? Write down the ways you can try to prevent being sick.

4. With friends, do an improvisation of people waiting in the doctor's office and talking about their weird ailments. Go in to the doctor and describe wild symptoms. The doctor has to diagnose the disease and come up with a remedy.

**Recording today:**
What illnesses or injuries have you had? What makes you feel better when you are sick?

**Imagining tomorrow:**
Imagine a twenty-first century in which all diseases can be cured or prevented. What would life be like if people didn't get sick? What would be the focus of the medical profession? Write about it, or draw what hospitals would be used for.

# The Right to Vote

Imagine going to vote and being told it was against the law, even though you are a citizen! Would you be mad? For almost 150 years, that's exactly what happened to any American woman who wanted to vote.

One of the most important rights of citizens in a democracy is the right to vote. But some people haven't had that right. That's called *suffrage.* In the American colonies, the only people who could vote were people who owned property. They were almost always men. In some colonies, only the people who went to one particular church could vote. After the American Revolution, the U.S. Constitution gave each state the power to decide who could vote. New Jersey was the only one of the first 13 states to say that women could vote. Then it took away that privilege again in 1807.

Many people, both men and women, protested against the unjust voting laws. A woman named Virginia Minor was one who was angry. When she tried to vote and couldn't, she took her case to the Supreme Court of the United States. But she lost. The court decided in 1872 that being a citizen did not give a woman the right to vote.

The fight for "woman suffrage" began in the early 1800s and went on for over a hundred years. In 1890, Wyoming let women vote; by 1918, fifteen states did. It finally took an amendment to the U.S. Constitution to open voting places (called polls) to the women of this country. In 1920, the Nineteenth Amendment gave voting rights to all American women.

African-Americans at one time did not have the right to vote, either. After the Civil War, two constitutional amendments in 1866 and 1870 made all former slaves citizens. This let African-American men vote—but not women, until 1920. Some Native Americans couldn't vote until 1948.

Even after the new laws passed, a few states found ways to keep some citizens from voting. They charged a poll tax or made requirements that not everyone could meet. In 1965, Dr. Martin Luther King, Jr. led a famous protest march in Selma, Alabama. Fifteen hundred Americans, both black and white, participated. Later that year, Congress passed the Voting Rights Act. Now all citizens of the United States can vote. But a lot of voters don't cast their ballots in an election. It's hard to understand why people who have the right to vote don't do it!

## Activities:

1. Think of ways your school class or club could help encourage people to vote. For example, make posters to put up in public places like a local store a few weeks before the next election. Call or write your community officials or the League of Women Voters to learn what else you might do to help get out the vote.

2. Find out about leaders in the fight for suffrage, such as Lucretia Mott, Elizabeth Cady Stanton, Lucy Stone, Susan B. Anthony, and Dr. Martin Luther King, Jr. Write and perform a play or puppet show in which they argue with the people who would like to keep others from having the right to vote.

3. The next time one of your parents or a grown-up friend votes, ask if you can go along to see what the voting process is like.

4. Try a family voting process. For a week, vote on everything: what to have for breakfast, when to go to bed, who should do certain chores, what TV to watch, etc. Practice making a motion, discussing it, and voting.

**Recording today:**
Write the names of your elected officials.

The President of the United States:

The Vice President:

The Senators from your state:

The Representative from your voting district:

The Governor of your state:

The Mayor of your city or town:

**Imagining tomorrow:**
People used to vote by writing their choice on a piece of paper and putting it in a box. Now most places have voting machines. Some are beginning to let people vote by mail. How do you think people will vote in the twenty-first century when you are of voting age?

# Chapter 6
## *This Earth*

# It's a Big World—Exploration and Discovery

Did you ever want to explore beyond your own house or yard? Then you can add your name to this list: Hennu and Hanno, Cartier and Chang Ch'ien, Alexander and Amerigo, Marco Polo and Magellan, Ericson and Amundsen. You too can be an explorer of the Earth.

People have always wondered what lies beyond their birthplace. As long as four thousand years ago, ancient civilizations explored the world in all directions. European and African explorers went west to England, south to Africa, and east to India. The Chinese explored Asia and the Middle East. Vikings traveled far west, and reached the coast of North America. Venetians went far east to China.

During the "Great Age of Discovery" in the 1400s, explorers from many countries competed to find the quickest routes for trade with other parts of the world. Racing to reach the Far East by ship, Christopher Columbus sailed west. Others looked for eastward routes. In the process, they discovered the Americas, found passages around Africa and South America, and made maps of much of the world—but not always accurately.

The Arctic and Antarctic were the last lands of Earth people explored. Many tried, but they usually failed because of the ice and cold temperatures. Commander Robert Peary led an expedition that finally reached the North Pole in 1909. Two years later, two groups competed to reach the South Pole. Roald Amundsen was the first to get there. The other expedition, led by Robert Falcon Scott, reached the Pole only to find Amundsen's Norwegian flag flying. Richard E. Byrd flew a small airplane over both Poles, in 1926 and 1929. In 1951 the atomic-powered submarine *Nautilus* sailed under the North Pole!

What makes human beings want to explore? Sometimes it's necessary for survival. People need to find new sources of food or safety from the weather or enemies. Sometimes we search for valuable resources such as oil, gold or silver, even water. Sometimes it's to increase trade with other people, or to persuade them to share our beliefs. There are other reasons too: human curiosity, our love of adventure, our desire to know more about the world.

Now that we have mapped the surface of the Earth, will exploration and discovery stop? Not while people exist! Unless human nature changes a lot, we will always look for new frontiers to explore.

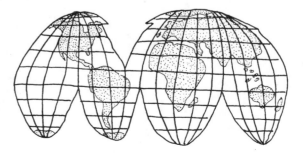

## Activities:

1. Explore a new kind of territory in your house or apartment: Holding a mirror to face the ceiling, imagine that what you see in the mirror is the floor. Take a walk around and see what it feels like to "walk" on your ceiling.

2. With your parents' permission, explore your neighborhood and write down everything you notice. What do you see, hear, feel, or smell that is typical of the neighborhood? What kind of buildings are there? What kinds of people, plants, animal life, and natural features do you find? As the discoverer, make an illustrated map of your neighborhood.

3. Make up an imaginary country and draw a map of it.

4. Act out or write about how the people in your imaginary country live.

**Recording today:**
Where have you traveled beyond your street or town? Write down all the places you have been since you were born.

*Imagining tomorrow:*
What might people explore in the twenty-first century? Write about or draw the kinds of vehicles they might use... or make a map of where they might find.

# New Frontiers—Ocean and Space

When people had made maps of all the lands on Earth, what was left to explore? What could satisfy our itch to discover the unknown?

One new frontier was the ocean, which covers more than 70 percent of the Earth. Hidden beneath all that water, the ocean floor had always been a place of mystery. What did it look like? What kind of animals and plants lived there? What could it tell us about Earth? The British ship *Challenger* made the first underwater survey in 1872–1876. They explored by dragging nets along the ocean bottom to bring up animals and plants. They dropped thermometers to measure ocean temperature and tested sea water. But  they still couldn't *see* what it was like under the ocean. That needed special equipment.

Diving suits, invented in the 1800s, let us get our first real peek into ocean life. But they were clumsy and dangerous. Jacques-Yves Cousteau's *aqualung*, in 1943, let people move around underwater more freely. Still, a diver's air supply lasts only a short time, and the great pressure of water limits how far down we can go. For long and deep explorations, the human body needs better protection. Submarines, diving spheres, and underwater laboratories make that possible. In 1930, William Beebe went one-half mile down in the *bathysphere*. The *bathyscaph*, invented in 1948 by Auguste Piccard, has let people go more than six miles underwater. Ocean exploration is still fascinating, and every year we learn more about this new frontier.

In the opposite direction from Earth's surface spreads another huge mystery: space. People have always looked at the sky and wondered what was up there. Early in the twentieth century, scientists started to experiment with rockets for space flight. After World War II, the United States and the Soviet Union (Russia) competed to be the first in space. Russia put up the first satellite, *Sputnik*, in 1957. Four months later, the United States launched its satellite, *Explorer*. A Russian cosmonaut, Yuri Gagarin, was the first man to go into space. Less than a month later, Alan Shepard made the first manned flight by the United States. More flights by both countries sent people up into space for longer and longer times. Then, in 1969, Neil Armstrong and Edwin Aldrin actually stepped onto the moon! That was the first of six moon explorations by American astronauts.

We've learned a lot about space, but there is much more to know. Today, most space research is done on space stations that circle the Earth permanently. The space shuttle, a vehicle that lifts off like a rocket but lands like an airplane, is used over and over again. We have also sent out unmanned rockets to explore other planets. They keep sending back information about this exciting, vast frontier, space.

BATHYSCAPH

## Activities:

1. Make your own space capsule. Find a big cardboard carton (the kind appliances come in works best). At one end, cut out a window and cover it with plastic wrap. Draw a control panel and make knobs and buttons. You can use the same capsule as a submarine to explore the ocean.

2. Draw a series of pictures of creatures you might see in the ocean. Copy pictures of real creatures, or invent your own. Or draw pictures of things you might encounter in space. Put them up in front of your space capsule or submarine.

3. With friends, take an imaginary trip to an unknown planet or to the bottom of the ocean. Arrange chairs to seat all the passengers. Take turns describing what you see along the way. If you're going to go out of the "space capsule" or "diving sphere," wear appropriate suits and helmets (paper bags with a hole cut out of the front work fine). Be sure to take along food for the trip.

4. Create a planet with an interesting surface: mountains, pits, etc. Sculpt it with modeling clay or dough made by mixing 2 cups flour, 2 tablespoons cooking oil, 1 cup water, and 1 cup salt. Add food coloring or paint if you want color.

**Recording today:**
What space explorations have been made during your lifetime? Ask your family or librarian to help you find out.

**Imagining tomorrow:**
Imagine yourself as an ocean or space explorer in the twenty-first century. Write about or draw what you would like to discover.

# On the Move

*Migration?* That word may make you think of birds flying south for the winter and back north for the summer. Many animals migrate. But people migrate too, moving from one place to another. We know that even before the story of humans was written down as history, people moved through the world. They went from Africa and Asia to Europe, from Asia to the Americas, and across all the continents.

The first Americans probably came here more than ten thousand years ago. They crossed from Asia on a "land bridge" near what today is Alaska. Then they moved south and east across the American continent. One of the most interesting mysteries of human migration is the puzzle of the Anasazi. These early Native Americans built pueblo-style villages and became farmers. They lived in many parts of the Southwest, in cliff houses at Mesa Verde in Colorado, and adobe towns in Arizona and New Mexico. Then they left. Why? Was it lack of rain? Disease? Enemies?

We can't be sure why the early human migrations took place, but we know that people move for many reasons. Changes in climate may make it too cold or too hot for them to live comfortably where they did. Food crops can fail if the weather changes. Sometimes food becomes scarce because a population grows too big for the area that supplies it. Other resources that a society depends on, like fresh water or fuel, may run out. Natural disasters like floods and volcanoes can also force people to move. Unfortunately, the worst side of human nature has sometimes played a part in migration. Slavery took people away from their homes against their will. Wars have forced people to flee and seek safety in new lands.

One of the biggest reasons for people to migrate is the desire to make their way of life better. They

try to find a place that offers opportunities that their homeland doesn't. The history of the United States is the story of this kind of migration. Beginning in 1607, people came to the American continent looking for a chance to improve their lives financially and to seek political or religious freedom. At first, most of the immigrants to America were from European countries, but in the 1900s, people began to come from all over the world.

That background of immigration makes our country rich in the traditions from cultures all across the globe. All the people who have come to this country have added to our arts, our food, our language, and our way of looking at the world.

## Activities:

1. When did your family come to the United States? What countries did they come from? Why? Write the countries down and mark them on a map of the world.

2. Talk to someone in your family or neighborhood who has come to this country from another place. Find out how it felt to move to another country. Ask them to describe their journey. Write down as many stories as they can tell you.

3. Learn what kind of food people eat in a part of the world that particularly interests you. Find a recipe that looks good and make it for your family, either alone or with help.

4. Write a story or a skit about a child who has to move to another country. What toys would the child want to take along?

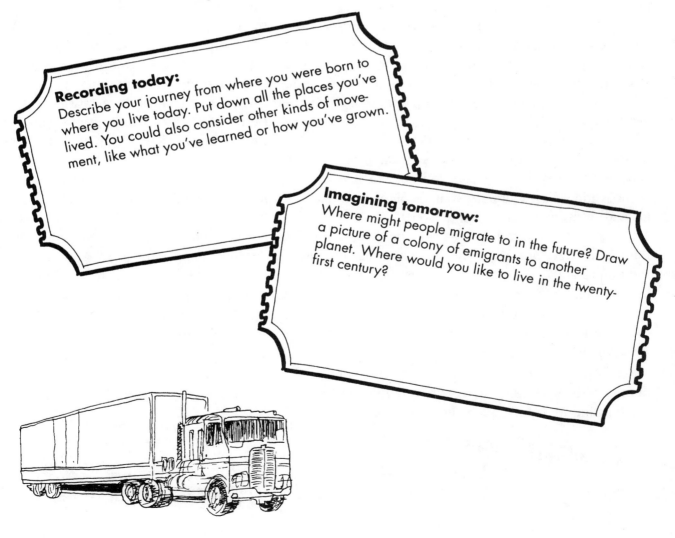

**Recording today:**
Describe your journey from where you were born to where you live today. Put down all the places you've lived. You could also consider other kinds of movement, like what you've learned or how you've grown.

**Imagining tomorrow:**
Where might people migrate to in the future? Draw a picture of a colony of emigrants to another planet. Where would you like to live in the twenty-first century?

# City or Country?

Do you remember the story of the city mouse and the country mouse? When the country mouse visited his cousin in the city, he was impressed by the city lifestyle. There was so much variety, so much food. Then, with shock, he discovered its danger—the house cat! Both cousins decided they liked their own place to live best.

Earth started out as a country place. There weren't many people, and their way of life depended on getting food. First they hunted animals and gathered grains. Then they learned to farm. These people often formed little villages for protection. Soon, villages started trading things with each other.

People began to build cities to make trade easier. Those cities were usually near water, because goods were sent by ship. (If you look at a map of the world, you will find most of the older cities located on rivers, oceans, or large lakes.) The earliest cities started around 3500 B.C. in what is now Iraq. Others developed in Egypt about 3000 B.C., in India about 2500 B.C., in China about 1500 B.C., and in the Americas about 200 B.C.

Gradually, over the centuries, cities grew. Most of them had walls to keep out enemies. Often they stood on a hill for even more protection. By the Middle Ages, cities were an important center of human activity. During the day, they were noisy and bustling. At night, though, they were quiet and dark. Curfews and the fear of crime kept everyone inside their houses.

The biggest growth of cities has been recent in the world's history. In 1850, less than 7 percent of the world lived in towns or cities of more than five thousand people. During the Industrial Revolution, new factories drew many to the cities to work. City populations grew. By 1950, over 60 percent of people in industrial countries like Japan and the United States lived in urban areas. That number keeps on growing. In some countries, the population of cities doubles every ten years! At the same time, many people have moved out of cities. Better transportation systems make it possible for people to work in the city, but live outside in suburbs.

People choose to live in the city for many reasons. Cities usually offer more jobs and different kinds of work. They have lots of stores and a wide choice of cultural events like concerts, plays, and museums. Some people find city life exciting, because of its fast pace and the activities they can choose to do. But others think cities are noisy, dirty, crowded, and dangerous. They prefer to live in smaller towns, or in the country, where it is cleaner and quieter, and they can have more privacy.

Which are you: a country mouse, a city mouse, or a suburban mouse?

76

## Activities:

1. Build your own temporary "town." Ask if you can have a place in the house that won't have to be cleaned out for a couple of weeks. Create a city out of boxes, toys, blocks, any odds and ends you can build with. Make roads with cars on them and put in trains and anything else you can think of. For a larger city, use sturdy cardboard cartons to make houses, churches, stores, schools, restaurants, theaters, museums, libraries, and other buildings.

2. How would the perfect city be laid out? Make a plan for the city of your dreams. What would it have in it? Besides all the buildings, plan places for recreation and sports, roads, and other types of transportation. Model it in clay or dough if you like.

3. Picture your ideal place to live, either in the country or a city. You can combine what you like best of both! Make a scrapbook of pictures you cut out of magazines to show what it is like.

**Recording today:**
Do you live in the country, city, town, or suburb? Tell about where you live and what you like about it.

**Imagining tomorrow:**
Write about or draw a picture of the city of the twenty-first century. What kind of buildings, recreation, and transportation will it have?

# Where Do You Get that Energy?

Think of yourself as a kind of machine. To keep going, you need fuel in the form of food and water. If you don't get enough fuel, you can run out of energy. Real machines are like that, too. They need fuel if they're going to run. Their fuel, like yours, usually comes from something in nature. That fuel creates the energy or power that makes the machine go.

Windmills, invented in the 600s, were one of the earliest machines to capture energy from na-  ture. They change wind into power to pump water or turn heavy millstones for grinding grain into flour. Water power is even older. The ancient Greeks made water wheels that used the energy of running water to turn grindstones. Animals walking on treadmills have also created the power to turn wheels. For thousands of years, wind, water, and animals were our major sources of power.

Then the Industrial Revolution changed the world. In the late 1700s, a Scottish engineer named James Watt invented the first practical engine that ran on the power of steam. Steam engines work when steam from boiling water moves a piston in and out. We've used those machines to pump water, run locomotive engines, drive ships, and do many other jobs.

Once we found out what engines could do, people began to make them do all sorts of work. Then we needed new sources of energy to run the engines. Toward the end of the nineteenth century, we began to depend more and more on electric energy, the source of power for electric lights and most of our appliances. We make (*generate*) electricity by turning other forms of power into electric energy. The power from water, wind, heat, and atomic energy can all be changed into electrical power.

Another kind of engine, the internal combustion engine, uses gasoline as fuel. We get gas from petroleum. Coal and petroleum are called *fossil fuels* because they come from plants that grew on Earth ages ago. Today fossil fuels make cars, trucks, and propeller airplanes go. We burn them to run engines, heat buildings, and make electricity. But some day the supply of fossil fuels will run out, so scientists are trying to find new sources of energy. Atomic energy promises clean and efficient power. Methane gas, made from garbage, will soon be able to run cars.

Still, we look for ways to improve old energy sources. Today we capture *solar* energy from the sun and *thermal* energy from the heat inside the Earth. Animals, wind, water, sun, electricity, fossil fuels, or atomic energy—nature is still the source of all our power.

## Activities:

1. To see the power of wind, make a pinwheel. Take an absolutely square piece of thin cardboard (about six inches square) and draw lines from corner to corner. Lay a penny in the middle and trace around it. Cut on the diagonal lines, stopping at the circle in the middle. Bend every other corner in to the center and fasten them with a pin. Then put the pin into the eraser at the end of a pencil.

2. Test the force of wind by flying a kite. What kind of wind do you need?

3. Dream up a new source of energy (squirrels running on a wheel, a new kind of windmill, etc.) Write an ad to "sell" your idea.

4. Experiment with static electricity. Blow up a balloon and rub it on clean dry hair for about thirty seconds. Then see what you can make follow the balloon. Try hair, little pieces of paper, bubbles, a Ping-Pong ball, puffed rice, a stream of running water from the tap.

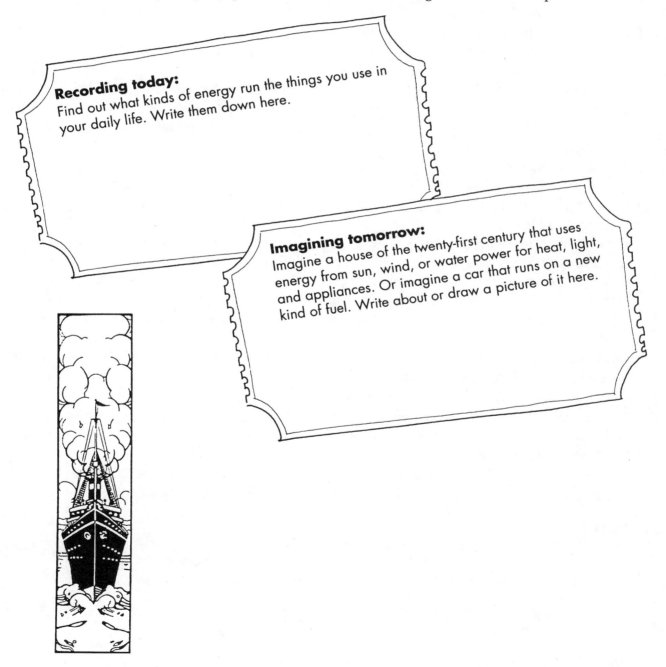

**Recording today:**
Find out what kinds of energy run the things you use in your daily life. Write them down here.

**Imagining tomorrow:**
Imagine a house of the twenty-first century that uses energy from sun, wind, or water power for heat, light, and appliances. Or imagine a car that runs on a new kind of fuel. Write about or draw a picture of it here.

# Earth, Our Home

Have you seen pictures of Earth that astronauts took? It's a beautiful blue and white ball floating against the dark of space. How are we going to make sure it always stays so lovely?

When the first settlers came to North America, they found a land of rich green forests and sparkling rivers and streams alive with animals. In the north, people could pick up lobsters by hand right off the beach. America seemed to promise endless natural resources for the people who came here, and for the countries they had left.

At first, traders sent back animal skins. Buffalo, deer, mink, fox, wolf, bear, muskrat, otter, raccoon, beaver—all those animals were hunted and trapped for their valuable skins. Beavers were killed in America to make hats for fashionable men in England!

Gradually, Americans learned just how much the continent had to give us. Forests provided lumber to make wood products and buildings. A plentiful supply of water made power for the machines of the industrial age. We mined coal to heat buildings and run those machines. We dug iron ore to make steel and used that to build bridges, railroad tracks, machines, skyscrapers, and cars. We found copper, silver, and gold. We found petroleum, from which we get gasoline, heating oil, and other products.

So what's the problem? Well, all those machines and factories and cars started to fill the air with smoke and other pollutants. We dumped harmful things into rivers and lakes. Both air and water were getting dirty. Some animals and plants began to disappear. Because our resources seemed endless, people threw too many things away instead of repairing or reusing them. We cut down more and more of our forests, and we burned too much gasoline. We grew careless about littering our neighborhoods and roads. As the population grew, this got worse and worse. Now, we are realizing that we have to keep our air and water clean and protect our resources.

America is not the only country that needs to work to save the Earth's environment. But it's the one where we can make a difference, today. And that will make tomorrow much better for us, for our children, and for all the animals and plants on Earth.

## Activities:

1. Make a "Tree Saver" box for your home or school to collect paper for recycling. Take a sturdy cardboard box. Label it TREE SAVER and decorate it by painting or pasting on pictures of nature cut out of magazines. Put it next to a trash can to remind everyone to recycle.

2. Make a poster about littering or recycling to put up in your school or local store.

3. Take the Earth Day Pledge (see below) with your classmates, club, or friends. Talk about what you can do to fulfill the pledge. Can you start a campaign to keep your town clean?

4. Write a letter to your governor, senator, or representative, urging them to support environmental issues.

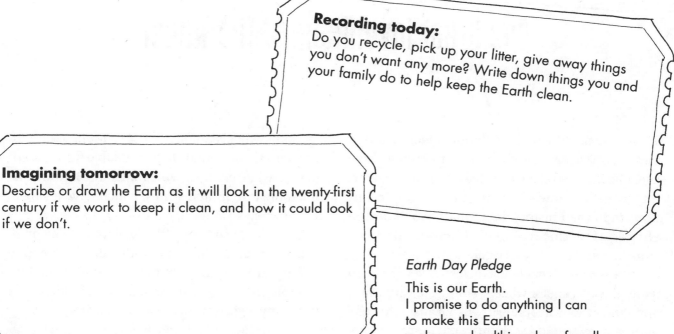

**Recording today:**
Do you recycle, pick up your litter, give away things you don't want any more? Write down things you and your family do to help keep the Earth clean.

**Imagining tomorrow:**
Describe or draw the Earth as it will look in the twenty-first century if we work to keep it clean, and how it could look if we don't.

*Earth Day Pledge*

This is our Earth.
I promise to do anything I can
to make this Earth
a cleaner, healthier place for all.
I promise to recycle,
not to litter,
and to love the trees and animals
on this Earth.

I realize that if I break my promise,
the Earth could be in much worse shape
than it is now.

Most of all, I promise to help the Earth
be the wonderful,
beautiful place it can be
if we all work together.

—Judith McNally

How to Help Keep the Earth Beautiful
- Give away or sell the good toys, books, clothes, or household items your family doesn't use any more.
- Don't litter.
- Find out how your community recycles paper, aluminum, and plastic—and do it.
- Use washable dishes and cloth napkins instead of plastic or paper.
- Cut down on the use of plastics and polystyrene.
- Use both sides of the paper when you write or draw.

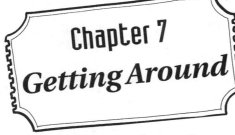
# One Great Invention—The Wheel

Try to imagine the world without wheels! Hard to picture, isn't it? Look around and notice how people use wheels to move themselves and their things. The wheel was one of the most important inventions in human history, more than five thousand years ago. Ever since then, people have used wheels to get around and to carry goods.

The earliest wheeled vehicles were carts with two slices of a log for wheels. They were very heavy and clumsy. Soon people learned that an open wheel with spokes would let them carry more and get around faster. Animals—oxen and cattle at first, then mules and horses—pulled the carts. Later, four-wheeled carts, or wagons, could carry even heavier loads. Over many centuries, the only real improvements were new ways to hitch the animals, and springs that made a carriage ride more comfortable.

Then engines were invented. People began to create new vehicles using new kinds of power. Steam engines provided the first power for trains, trucks, buses, tractors, and automobiles. In the 1880s, two Germans, Karl Benz and Gottlieb Daimler, began to make cars with internal combustion engines. They ran on gasoline. That decision changed the transportation systems of the world forever. It led to the development of today's high-speed cars, elaborate highway systems, and (alas) the traffic jam.

Some wheels are just for fun. Young children play with scooters and wagons. People have glided on four-wheeled roller skates since 1863. Now, lots of people love in-line skates, which have a single row of wheels.

America fell in love with the bicycle a long time ago. At the Philadelphia Exhibition of 1876, people saw an "ordinary English bicycle" and wanted it. That bicycle had a front wheel five feet high and a tiny eighteen-inch rear wheel. Only eight years later, fifty thousand Americans were riding bicycles. By the 1890s, there were ten million cyclists! By then the bicycle was safer, with two wheels of about the same size. People formed "touring clubs" to take bicycle trips together. The popular *tandem* bikes, for two people, could have two, three, or four wheels. Bicycle racing started in 1883, and within ten years it was a real fad. Today almost everyone knows how to ride a bike, and bicycle races and trips are more popular than ever.

Of course, we love motors, so we had to invent the motorcycle, too. It started out in 1868 as a bicycle with a steam engine attached under the seat. What's next? Roller skates with an engine?

## Activities:

1. Re-create the first wheels. Push a book along a row of evenly spaced pencils and see how the round "wheels" move it along easily.

2. Make your own crazy cart, scooter, or car. Use discarded wheels from bicycles, wagons, even old roller skates. Make the body from scraps of wood, cartons, chair seats, or whatever you can find.

3. Write a story or put on a play or puppet show about the invention of the wheel. Invent fun names for the characters and why they had to invent the wheel. What were those first wheels like?

4. How many kinds of wheeled vehicles have you ridden in during your lifetime? List them. Don't forget when you were a baby!

**Recording today:**
Look around your house, yard, and garage. How many things do you find that have wheels? Write them all down here.

**Imagining tomorrow:**
What new kinds of wheeled transportation can you imagine for the twenty-first century? Draw or write about some possibilities, either for practical use or for fun.

# The Horseless Carriage

*Get a horse!* People used to tease early motorists when their automobile broke down or got stuck in the mud. But that didn't stop anybody who had fallen madly in love with the newest rage. People felt adventurous and glamorous when they put on special coats, goggles, hats, and scarves, and drove off in their *horseless carriage.*

The first cars in the late 1800s ran by steam. Steam cars were dirty, noisy, and scary. They had open fires and hot steam blowing around. Electric cars were quieter, but they couldn't go very far or very fast. During the 1890s, people in many countries experimented with cars that ran on gasoline engines. That was the kind of car that finally changed the world.

The early days of motoring were exciting times in America. Those first cars weren't too sturdy, and a driver had to be prepared to repair tires, engines, or whatever might break down. Roads were dirt, meant to be used by horses. Motorists often found themselves blinded by dust or stuck deep in mud. Some doctors warned that driving would cause mental disturbance and problems with blood circulation! Still, in 1900, eight thousand people owned automobiles.

At first, cars were very expensive, and only the rich could afford them. In 1908, Henry Ford began to make a car that most people could buy. He called it the Model T, but it usually went by a nickname like the *flivver* or *Tin Lizzie.* Model T's were easy to drive, and most people could repair them when they broke down. By 1910, four million of them were on the roads of America. The 1920s saw improvements in those roads. By then it was clear that cars were here to stay. By the 1930s, automobile travel had become a major part of American life.

Then came World War II. We stopped making cars during the war because factories had to build ships, tanks, and other war machines. Gasoline and rubber for tires were rationed, so people couldn't drive much. Many people put their cars in storage. When the war ended, America's passion for the automobile blossomed once more. Families went out for Sunday drives, at first in their old prewar autos. Then the new cars of the 1950s came out. They dazzled everyone, with their long bodies and sculptured "fins." Some had three different colors! But those cars also ate up a lot of fuel. In the 1970s, gasoline shortages and people's interest in the environment made smaller cars popular. It became fashionable to drive a "VW Bug," the smallest car on the road.

The automobile changed American life more than any other invention. When people had cars, they could move easily from place to place. Cities spread out and suburbs grew. Small towns were no longer isolated places. People felt more independent. Still, many people are now dependent on their car!

## Activities:

1. When did your parents and grandparents learn to drive? What kinds of cars have they had in their lives?

2. Take an imaginary car ride. Find a section of a map with fun names of towns you can go through. Write a story about your trip. Or do the trip with friends and improvise a play as you go along. Tell what you see and what you are doing as you go.

3. Make a collection of cars, either old ones or new ones. Draw them or cut out pictures from magazines for a scrapbook.

4. Create a funny new car. Take a toy car and change it by painting or pasting on feathers, ribbons, sequins, and other things.

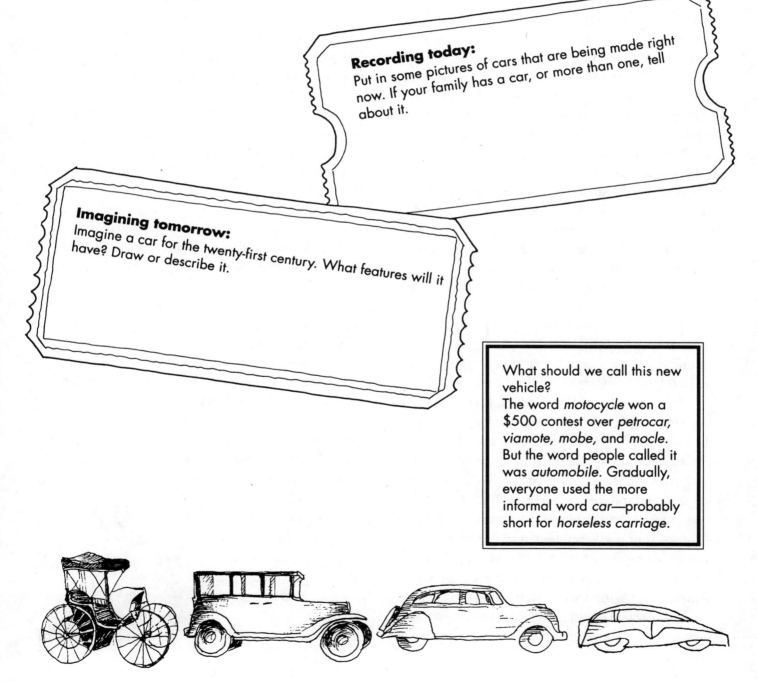

**Recording today:**
Put in some pictures of cars that are being made right now. If your family has a car, or more than one, tell about it.

**Imagining tomorrow:**
Imagine a car for the twenty-first century. What features will it have? Draw or describe it.

What should we call this new vehicle?
The word *motocycle* won a $500 contest over *petrocar*, *viamote*, *mobe*, and *mocle*. But the word people called it was *automobile*. Gradually, everyone used the more informal word *car*—probably short for *horseless carriage*.

# The Iron Horse

Let's go back to 1870 and take a trip on that wonderful recent invention, the railroad train. We call it the "iron horse" because it replaces the animals we depended on for so long to carry us around. When you hear that whistle blow, all you have to do is buy yourself a ticket. Hop aboard, settle down in your plush seat, and give the conductor your yellow ticket to punch. It's that easy to join the company of great adventurers!

Who ever thought up the idea of a train? Since the 1500s, animals and people dragged carts along tracks, usually to haul coal in mines. Then, in 1803, Richard Trevithick invented a locomotive powered by steam. It chugged along at only five miles an hour. In 1814, George Stephenson designed a locomotive that could pull trains on a railroad track. The first real railway opened in England in 1822. It carried both passengers and freight over a track just twenty-five miles long. Soon America, too, began to build tracks for trains.

Railroads changed our country. They opened it up for people to move around and to ship goods. In 1869, the first rail line clear across the United States was finished. Before that, it was very hard to go from the East to the West coast. A trip across the country by land was long, exhausting, and dangerous. Animals had to pull wagons over rough trails. The weather was often bad, and there were huge mountain ranges to cross. If you went by ship, you had to go all the way around the tip of South America. Imagine what a difference the railroad made! Now you could relax and enjoy the scenery while you ate your meals in the dining car or sat in the parlor car. You could sleep in a Pullman car, with seats that turned into a bunk bed.

We still ship goods around the country by train. You may have seen a long freight train pulled by two or more locomotives. They have many different kinds of cars, designed for different goods. Flatcars, boxcars, tank cars, refrigerator cars, and open-top hopper cars are some of them. Last of all comes the caboose, a car for the crew that works on the train.

American folk music is full of songs about great heroes of railroading, like Casey Jones. He was a real person, an engineer who had a reputation for fast driving and for the unusual way he could blow his train's whistle. Casey died in a train wreck, and before long he was the hero of a famous song. Other songs remember "steel drivers" like John Henry, who worked making railroad tunnels, and famous trains like the "Wabash Cannonball." Many people don't know that "She'll Be Comin' Around the Mountain" is a song about trains.

Steam engines were fun to watch with their puffs of smoke and their hissing and chuffing noises. Faster, cleaner diesel-electric locomotives began to replace steam engines in the 1920s. Now high-speed trains, like Japan's "bullet train," can go at speeds of up to 130 miles per hour.

*All Aboard!* Let's go!

## Activities:

1. Read about some famous trains, or talk to someone who took a train trip in the past. Find out what it was like. Where did they sleep and eat? What were the seats like?

2. Learn some folk songs about railroads. (You can find books of folk songs in your library.) Write a new verse for one song.

3. Draw pictures to illustrate one of the songs or draw an old train from a picture in a book.

4. Write a story, poem, or play about a ride on a train.

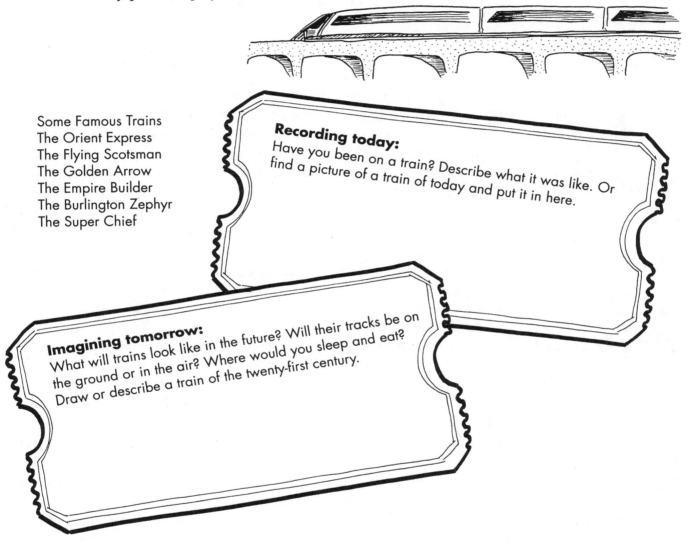

Some Famous Trains
The Orient Express
The Flying Scotsman
The Golden Arrow
The Empire Builder
The Burlington Zephyr
The Super Chief

**Recording today:**
Have you been on a train? Describe what it was like. Or find a picture of a train of today and put it in here.

**Imagining tomorrow:**
What will trains look like in the future? Will their tracks be on the ground or in the air? Where would you sleep and eat? Draw or describe a train of the twenty-first century.

Some Folk Songs About Trains

"Nine Hundred Miles"
"John Henry"
"Casey Jones"
"Paddy Works on the Erie"
"O, Lula!"
"Can'cha Line 'Em"
"The Big Rock Candy Mountains"

"She'll Be Comin' Around the Mountain"
"A Railroader for Me"
"Jerry, Go an' Ile that Car"
"Drill, Ye Tarriers"
"Wand'rin'"
"Around a Western Water Tank"
"The Wabash Cannonball"

(These songs can be found in *Folk Song U.S.A.* by John and Alan Lomax.)

(These songs can be found in *The Folk Songs of North America* by Alan Lomax.)

# Down to the Sea in Ships

Egyptian ship
c. 2500 B.C.

Caravel
15th Century

Whaler
19th Century

"Clermont"
1807

How do you get around? On foot? On a bike? In a car? The earliest kind of transportation was by water. As long ago as 8000 B.C., someone watched logs floating down a river and got the idea to hollow out a log and ride in it. That was the first boat, called a *dugout canoe.*

By 7250 B.C., countries around the Mediterranean Sea started to trade things with each other across the water. Lots of people rowed hard to move those first ships. At some point, sailors discovered that they could use the wind to make their ships go. By 3000 B.C. the ancient Egyptians were using sails as well as oars on reed boats that went up and down the Nile River.

The first sailboats needed the wind to blow from behind them. This meant that sailors had to wait until the wind was coming from the right direction before they could go anywhere. Gradually, people developed sails they could turn to let ships move in the direction they wanted, no matter where the wind came from. The earliest movable sails were triangular, called *lateen sails.* Later ships had sails of other shapes. A *full-rigged*

ship might have as many as twenty-six sails of different sizes and shapes.

Ships changed dramatically after James Watt invented the steam engine. In 1801, William Symington of England built a steam-powered boat named the *Charlotte Dundas.* The first passenger steamer was the *Clermont,* built by the American Robert Fulton. Steamships crossed the oceans for many years, carrying passengers and goods. Today most cargo ships have diesel engines. The first nuclear-powered cargo ship, the *Savannah,* went into service in 1962.

Submarines were developed as warships. They can move underwater and stay under for a long time. A submarine with nuclear power can go completely around the world without once coming to the surface!

When humans go anywhere, we like to go fast. Speedboats are a favorite form of water recreation. Other kinds of boats go fast, too. A *hydrofoil* has wings that lift the bottom (*hull*) out of the water when it reaches full speed. This makes it able to go much faster than most boats. A *hovercraft* can skim on a cushion of air over either water or land. It can go places ordinary boats can't, like swamps.

Today's road systems are very advanced, and we can fly quickly over long distances, but even now we depend on water. It's usually cheapest to send goods from one country to another by ship. Besides, most people love boats. Give us a rowboat, a canoe, a motorboat, even a paddleboat, and we're like ducks in water!

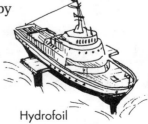

Hydrofoil

## Activities:

1. In the sink or bathtub, experiment with what floats. Take several gum wrappers and pieces of paper and try them flat, scrunched up, folded into different shapes. (A folded paper hat makes a good boat.) Try other things of different weight and shapes. Which is more important, weight or shape?

2. Make a walnut shell boat. Put a little piece of clay inside a walnut shell half. Cut out a sail about the size of a postage stamp. Stick a toothpick in and out of the sail for a mast, and put the bottom of it in the clay. Have a race with several boats.

3. Go on an imaginary cruise around the world. Send back postcards from the ports you visit. Use five-by-seven-inch index cards. Put pictures on one side (draw them or cut them from magazines). On the other side, tell what you're doing in that place. Don't forget to address it!

4. Make a submarine from large cardboard cartons. Put two cartons end to end so you can crawl through them, and tape them together. Stand a somewhat larger one upright next to them and attach it. (It should be big enough for you to sit up in.) That will be the conning tower. Attach one more carton on the other side of the tower. Cut doors in the tower carton at the height of the other ones so you can go all the way through. Make a periscope from a paper towel tube.

**Recording today:**
What kind of boat or ship have you been on? Tell about it here. If you never have, tell about what kind you'd like to go on.

**Imagining tomorrow:**
What will ships be like in the twenty-first century? Imagine the uses or design of a ship of the future and draw or write about it.

# It's a Bird, It's a Plane

Did you ever wish you could fly? Everyone does! One of the oldest stories in the world is the Greek myth of Daedelus. He made wings out of feathers and wax, and flew. His son,  Icarus, flew too close to the sun. The wax melted, and Icarus fell out of the sky.

Over the centuries, humans have tried over and over to find a way to fly. At first, they tried to imitate birds by fastening wings onto their arms. But people aren't built like birds, and this didn't work. We still envied birds, though. We made up our word for flight, *aviation*, from *avis*, the Latin word for bird.

The first real aviation triumph was the hot-air balloon. In 1783, the Montgolfier brothers of France traveled five miles—an amazing accomplishment! 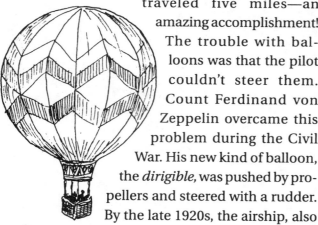 The trouble with balloons was that the pilot couldn't steer them. Count Ferdinand von Zeppelin overcame this problem during the Civil War. His new kind of balloon, the *dirigible*, was pushed by propellers and steered with a rudder. By the late 1920s, the airship, also called a *zeppelin*, was making regular flights across the Atlantic Ocean.

But the airplane was a safer and better machine. People had been sailing in aircraft with wings, called *gliders*, since the 1890s. Then two brothers, Orville and Wilbur Wright, made a flying machine that had a motor. The Wright brothers made the first successful airplane flight in 1903, at Kitty Hawk, North Carolina. We might call it a hop. It went only 120 feet and lasted just twelve seconds! After that flight, airplane design improved quickly. Only sixteen years later, in 1919, a plane flew across the Atlantic Ocean! Before long, travelers were flying on regular airline flights. Mail delivery speeded up when letters went by plane instead of truck or train. Planes with jet engines, invented in the 1950s, flew much faster than the old propeller engines. Today, supersonic airplanes can fly faster than the speed of sound.

Another kind of aircraft is the helicopter, first built in 1936. It can take off and land straight up and down. Airplanes need a long runway for take-offs and land-  ings. Helicopters can go in and out of many places that planes can't. Some newer aircraft can take off like a helicopter and then fly like an airplane.

Space flight is the latest triumph of human desire to rise above the Earth. People first flew into space in 1961. The first Russian and American flights were very short. But only eight years later, two American astronauts, Neil Armstrong and Edwin Aldrin, set foot on the moon. Today, American flights into space use the space shuttle, a reusable aircraft. It takes off like a rocket but lands like an airplane. What will we invent to take us even farther into the air?

## Activities:

1. Try out different kinds of paper airplanes and gliders. Which kind works best? Invent your own paper plane. Have a competition with a friend to see whose goes farthest.

2. In a shoebox, make a diorama of a historic flight: a balloon, a dirigible, the Wright brothers' first airplane flight, a rocket going into space.

3. With friends, improvise a play about an airplane flight. Set up chairs for passengers and pilots. Act out what's happening as the flight goes on. Don't forget the flight attendants or the food! You could even have a "bon voyage" party before you "take off."

4. When did your parents or grandparents take their first airplane flights? What was air travel like when they were young? Make a list of all the space flights or new inventions in aircraft that have taken place since you were born.

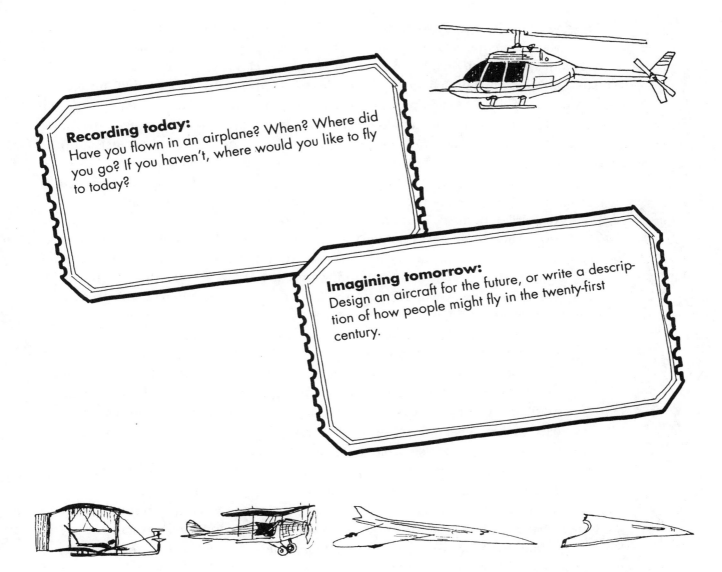

**Recording today:**
Have you flown in an airplane? When? Where did you go? If you haven't, where would you like to fly to today?

**Imagining tomorrow:**
Design an aircraft for the future, or write a description of how people might fly in the twenty-first century.

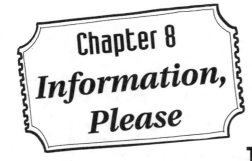

# Chapter 8
# Information, Please

# The Written Word

Imagine yourself on a day when an amazing thing has happened to you. You want to tell someone, but nobody is around. You don't have a telephone, a computer, not even paper, pen, or ink. Worse, there is no alphabet. There's no way you can write that news down, not even to save it for yourself to remember later.

That was the situation of the earliest humans. The only way they could pass on an experience, idea, or story was to say it aloud to someone else. We just had to invent writing!

Early people would cut notches on sticks, or tie knots in strings, to keep track of numbers. Sometimes they made drawings on rocks to leave each other simple messages. It was a natural next step for people to start putting pictures together in a series. Then they could tell a more elaborate story or send a longer message. The first written symbols were drawings, called *ideographs* or *pictographs*. All people could understand a picture, no matter what language they spoke.

The Sumerians invented *cuneiform*, a system of picture writing, sometime before 3000 B.C. On a slab of wet clay, they scratched symbols that could stand for a word or for a syllable. Around the same time, ancient Egyptians created another kind of ideographs, called *hieroglyphics*. The ancient Chinese developed the most complicated of all picture writing systems. It had as many as fifty thousand symbols. Compare that with the twenty-six letters you had to learn before you could write!

One trouble with ideographs is that it takes so many pictures to tell something. And how do you draw a picture of a word like "the"? We needed a new kind of writing that would say things in a better way. Instead of drawing pictures of objects, people started to use symbols that stood for an idea. To say "five stones," you could use a symbol that meant "five" and another that meant "stone." Later, the symbols came to stand for sounds instead of objects. Now, letters could be put together in different ways to write down any word you could say. Instead of memorizing the pictures for a lot of words, you only had to learn the few letters of an alphabet.

The word *alphabet* comes from the first two letters of the Greek alphabet, *alpha* and *beta*. The symbols we use today for writing and printing are very old. But the alphabet is one of the first things little children learn. It's our key to the world of reading and writing.

## Activities:

1. With a friend, invent your own system of hieroglyphics, and send each other messages to decode.

2. A rebus is a puzzle that replaces words with pictures of things that sound like those words. Amuse your friends with a rebus you invent.

3. Practice mirror writing. Write or print backward, so that your message may be read in a mirror. It's tricky at first, but you can get the hang of it fairly quickly.

4. Some people think English spelling should be changed because words are often not pronounced the way they're spelled. For example, "they're," "their," and "there" are pronounced the same but spelled differently. The words "bough," "rough," "cough," and "through" are spelled similarly but pronounced differently. Take a paragraph from a book and change the spellings so that the words look the way they sound.

**Recording today:**
Write a message here for yourself to read when you are older. What do you want to tell that future you about yourself today?

**Imagining tomorrow:**
Would you change our alphabet? Are there letters we don't need? Are there letters we do need for special sounds that we don't have? Imagine an alphabet for the future. Write a sentence using it.

# Writing—Tools of the Trade

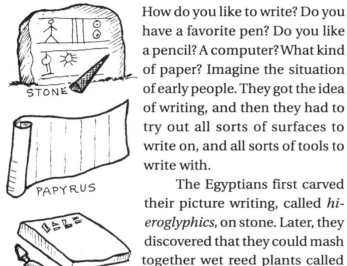

STONE

PAPYRUS

CLAY

PARCHMENT

How do you like to write? Do you have a favorite pen? Do you like a pencil? A computer? What kind of paper? Imagine the situation of early people. They got the idea of writing, and then they had to try out all sorts of surfaces to write on, and all sorts of tools to write with.

The Egyptians first carved their picture writing, called *hieroglyphics,* on stone. Later, they discovered that they could mash together wet reed plants called *papyrus* and spread the mash into a sheet. When it dried, they had a flat papery surface suitable for writing. The Sumerians scratched *cuneiform* symbols with a wedge-shaped tool on a slab of moist clay. Then they dried the clay to make it more lasting. Ancient Greeks and Romans wrote on soft wax tablets with an instrument made of metal or bone, called a *stylus.* In Palestine and Syria, early people wrote on leather. In ancient India, they used strips cut from palm leaves, or birch bark. Some people printed symbols on sheets of copper. *Parchment* is a beautiful writing surface made from thinly stretched and scraped skins of animals, especially sheep or goats. Because parchment lasts for a long time, people often used it for important documents. From the 300s until the mid-1400s, scribes copied books by hand on the finest parchment, called *vellum.* Then Gutenberg invented the printing press, which printed on paper.

The word *paper* comes from the Egyptian *papyrus.* Modern paper was invented by Ts'ai Lun in China in A.D. 105. News of this amazing product slowly spread to the rest of the world. Today, writing paper is usually made from rags or wood pulp, or both mixed together.

Modern people can pick from many kinds of writing tools. Here's how some of them developed.

THE PEN
Prehistoric: sharp bits of stone or metal, animal hairs
300 B.C. Egyptians: sharpened reed dipped in soot mixed with water
Ancient Greeks and Egyptians: hollow reeds with a sharp point, filled with ink
50 B.C.: Sharpened goose quills (*pen,* from Latin word *penna,* feather)
1650: Some pens of metal with jewels as the tip
1750: Dip pen of steel points fit into a holder
1884: Louis Waterman invented ink-filled fountain pen
1913: W. A. Schaeffer invented lever for filling fountain pen
1920s: disposable cartridges for fountain pens invented
1938: Lazlo Biro invented the ballpoint pen
1951: porous-tip markers invented

THE PENCIL
Ancient Greece and Rome: pieces of lead
1500s: graphite used instead of lead
1650: pencils of graphite in wood cases
1795: Nicolas Jacques Conte invented today's pencil-making process
1700s: first mechanical pencils

WRITING BY MACHINE
1874: Remington company produced first typewriter
early 1900s: first portable typewriter

1920s: first electric typewriter
1936: first automatic typewriter could store paragraphs
1964: IBM produced first word processor

## Activities:

1. Write notes to a friend in invisible ink, written with a toothpick dipped in lemon juice or vinegar. Let the "ink" dry. To read the message, hold the paper near a warm light bulb until the writing appears.

2. Create some writing tools from things around you: twigs, skewers, toothpicks, etc. Try making ink of different materials: soot mixed with water, crushed berries, mud, clay, dirt, ground-up soft stones, plants, drink crystals, colored chalks, ashes, coffee, tea.

3. Try cuneiform writing. Press shapes into a slab of modeling clay. Try different tools (a pencil, the decorative end of a pen, a popsicle stick, your fingernail, paper clips, kitchen gadgets, buttons, rubber bands, etc.) to see what creates the most interesting shapes.

4. Make paper.

> *To make recycled paper:* Tear newspapers into very small pieces and drop them in a bucket. When it's half full, add enough water to wet the pieces. Let it stand for at least two hours. Beat the mess to a creamy pulp with a whisk. Dissolve 3 tablespoons cornstarch in 1 cup water and mix into pulp. Take a piece of screen or wire mesh about six inches across. Submerge it in the mixture and lift out gently. Repeat until screen has one-eighth inch of pulp on it. Lay the screen on top of newspapers, cover with plastic wrap. Blot over plastic with a towel. Set screen up so air can dry the pulp.

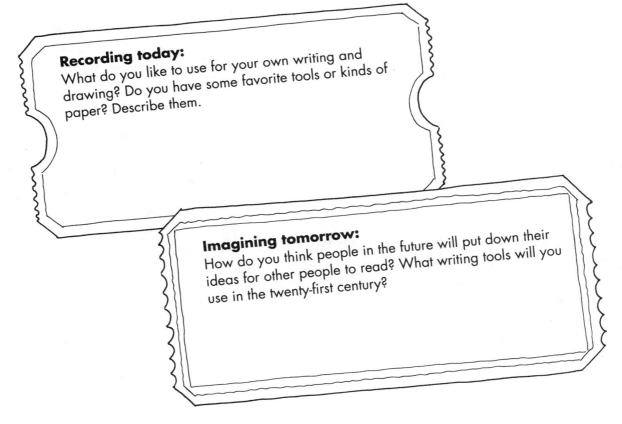

**Recording today:**
What do you like to use for your own writing and drawing? Do you have some favorite tools or kinds of paper? Describe them.

**Imagining tomorrow:**
How do you think people in the future will put down their ideas for other people to read? What writing tools will you use in the twenty-first century?

# The Art of the Book

Are you one of the lucky people who love books? Do you like the feel of them in your hands? Do you like the smell of a new book? When you open a book, do you like to look at the pictures and the way the words are printed?

Although it seems to us that printed books have been around forever, they haven't. For a long time, all books were handwritten. The Chinese made the first printed book in A.D. 868. It was on a long roll of paper, printed by carved wooden blocks covered with ink. A Chinese printer named Pi Sheng made the first movable type around 1045, out of hardened clay. Movable type is a great improvement over block print because letters can be arranged to make one page of writing, and then reused to make another.

Meanwhile, in Europe, scribes were still copying out every book by hand—a long, slow process. Some monks spent their whole lives copying and illustrating books with quill pens. Then, around 1450, Johannes Gutenberg invented a printing press with movable metal type. To print with his press, Gutenberg lined up letters to spell out words on a page of type. Then he covered the type with ink, put a piece of paper on top of the type, and lowered a heavy block on to it. A large screw pressed down on the block and printed the page. Gutenberg's press could print about sixteen pages an hour: much faster and more accurate than hand copying!

The printing press was one of the most important inventions in the history of the world. It encouraged people to become literate (able to read).

For the first time, knowledge was available to ordinary people. Gutenberg's first printed book was the Bible. Literature and scientific books have also been published from the beginning.

In 1886, the newly invented Linotype machine let printers set type mechanically rather than by hand. A process called *phototypesetting*, developed in 1939, was even faster. Today, words are typed into a computer and then printed on photographic paper. The computer has even made it possible for individual people to do "desktop publishing" and put out their own printed material.

Some people think that printing will disappear because of new technology that can store information in a smaller space. But books have the advantage of being easy to pick up and hold, and they are portable. It's not so comfortable curling up in a big chair with a computer!

## Activities:

1. Make a potato print. Cut a large potato in half. Draw a letter or a simple shape on it. Cut away the potato around the letter or shape. Dip the shape into poster paint and push it against a piece of paper to print. Or cut a shape into the potato and paint the flat part around the shape to print a white image on a colored oval. Try printing with small objects like bottle caps, spools, erasers, corks, buttons dipped into paint.

2. A rubbing is a kind of printing. Take a sheet of white paper and put it over something that has raised parts or a rough surface. For example: coins, leaves or bark, a license plate, rough fabric, concrete. Rub the paper with a crayon or the flat of a pencil and see the pattern that appears.

3. Try making sun prints. Take some construction paper or fax paper. Put objects on top in an interesting pattern. You could use shapes you cut out of other paper, keys, small toys, leaves, flowers, or other things. Weight them down so they won't blow around, and leave them in the sun all day. The paper will change color, leaving a design of the things that were on top of it.

4. Create your own book, a "Book of Today." Collect photographs, magazine pictures, favorite sayings or quotations, lists of things you like, things you didn't have room to include in this book. Include short descriptions of events or ideas you want to remember. Paste them on good paper and fasten the sheets together in a sturdy cover. Or use a scrapbook. Add to this as the year goes on.

**Recording today:**
What books do you own? Write them all here, or just write down your favorite books.

**Imagining tomorrow:**
Will there still be books when you are grown up? What will they be like? Describe the books of the twenty-first century.

# Talking Long Distance

How many times a day do you want to talk to someone who isn't with you? Imagine not being able to call your best friend—or order a pizza!

One early puzzle for humans was how they could communicate with each other at a distance. At first, people sent short messages by beating on logs or drums and signaling with whistles, smoke, or hilltop bonfires. These were the first *telecommunications*, (from the Greek word *tele,* meaning *far off).*

The *semaphore telegraph,* invented in 1794, sent messages from one tower to another by metal arms that moved to different positions. Towers spaced three to six miles apart could send a message ninety times as fast as a messenger on a horse. People in all countries worked hard to improve the telegraph. Finally, in the 1830s, Samuel F. B. Morse invented the Morse code. Now people could send messages, tapped out as dots and dashes, over an electric telegraph system.

One thing was missing, though: the human voice. People still wanted to have a real conversation. In 1876, Alexander Graham Bell invented a world-changing device: the telephone. Bell's first message calling his assistant went just to the next room. Before long, people could call from house to house.

In the early days of telephones, calls had to go through a *telephone exchange.* It was operated by a person who connected the

wire you were calling on to a wire for the person you were calling. That made phoning slow and limited the distance you could call. Today you can pick up your phone and instantly dial a number to speak with someone almost anywhere in the world. You can even call from a moving car, on a *cellular phone.*

Today's telephones use pretty much the same principles as the earliest ones. A voice talking into the phone makes air vibrate, and the vibrating air makes a thin flexible disk (a *diaphragm*) vibrate. That causes a vibration in an electric current, turning the sound into signals that are sent along a wire to another phone. There they are turned back into sound. One major improvement was the development of *optical fibers.* They turn the voice into flashes of light that travel along the fibers. Satellites have been used since 1963 to relay telephone messages across long distances.

Now we have a lot of new ways to communicate with each other. Since the 1980s, we can send words and pictures along telephone lines with a *facsimile machine,* usually called a *fax.* The biggest change, though, has been communication by computer. Now we can contact someone through *e-mail,* an international series of computer networks. If a computer is linked to the *Internet,* people can have typed-in conversations with others about anything they want.

## Activities:

1. Make a tin can telephone. Cut the lids off two cans. With a hammer and nail, punch a hole in the bottom of each can. Cut a piece of string about fifty feet long. Put an end of the string through the hole in each can. Tie a button to the end of the string inside each can so it won't pull out. To talk on the telephones, move far enough apart so that the string is pulled tight and doesn't touch anything. While one person talks into a can, the listener holds the other can to his/her ear. Vibrations in the tight string make the bottom of the can vibrate. You can also make a telephone by putting a funnel at each end of a garden hose to talk and listen.

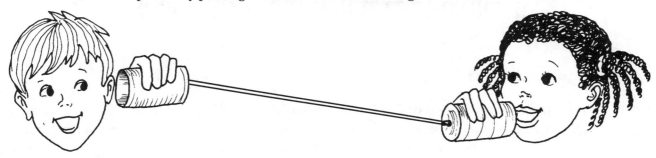

2. Learn the Morse code and practice sending messages by tapping them out with a spoon on an empty can.

3. With a friend, invent a code for sending messages. One simple kind of code is to substitute one letter for another. For example, A becomes X, B becomes M, C becomes G, etc. If both of you have a copy of your new "alphabet," you'll be able to send and read messages that nobody else can decode.

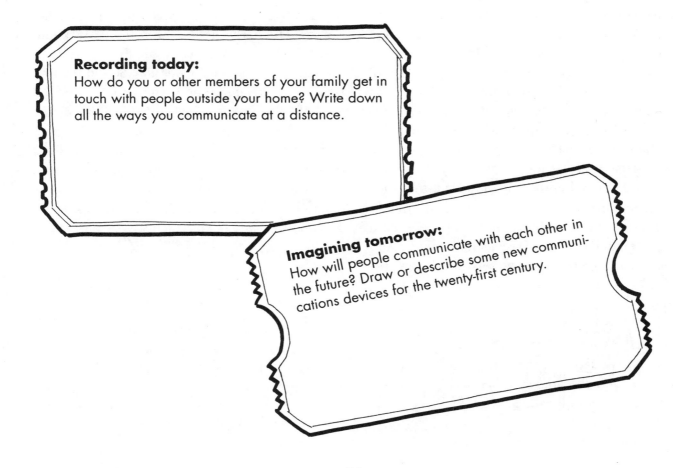

**Recording today:**
How do you or other members of your family get in touch with people outside your home? Write down all the ways you communicate at a distance.

**Imagining tomorrow:**
How will people communicate with each other in the future? Draw or describe some new communications devices for the twenty-first century.

# In the Air—Radio and Television

How often do you turn on the radio or TV? Most people do it at least once a day. We listen to radios at home, in our cars, on the beach, even working or exercising. We watch news and favorite entertainment programs on TV. Radio and television started as methods of communication, and they are still the fastest way to send messages. They both make use of *electromagnetic waves* that travel through space as fast as light.

In 1901, the Italian scientist Guglielmo Marconi invented a radio system that could send signals across the Atlantic Ocean. It let people communicate without having to build elaborate systems of electric wires. It wasn't long before someone thought, "Wow! If it sends messages so easily, we could use radio for entertainment, too."

*Broadcasting* means sending out programs that many people can hear at the same time. The first radio broadcast in the United States took place on Christmas Eve in 1906. It featured music, poems, and talk. When people found out that they could hear music over the air, they were dying to have a radio in their homes. Suddenly there was a huge demand for radio receivers. People could even make their own "crystal sets" to receive programs. By the 1920s, there were stations all over the country that broadcast shows for entertainment and information. Certain radio programs became very popular. During the 1930s and '40s, families would gather in the living room to listen to their favorite shows together.

A Scottish inventor, John Logie Baird, demonstrated television in 1926. The first TV program, broadcast in America in 1928, starred Felix the Cat. World War II slowed down the development of television broadcasting. It was only after the war, in the late 1940s, that many people had TV sets in their homes. The early pictures were only black and white, and not always very clear. Even so, TV immediately became really popular. So did the first families in a neighborhood to have a television set!

Color TV broadcasting started in 1953. By the 1980s, satellite receivers were common. TV programs are sent up and then down from satellites orbiting in space, and picked up by the receiver. Now, with video recorders, we can tape TV shows to play back later, or rent or buy videotapes at special stores.

## Activities:

1. Make your own "TV set" for live programs. Take a large sturdy cardboard box (appliance boxes are best) and cut out the front to be the screen. Cut a door in the back and put on your own TV programs from inside the box. Make a remote "zapper" out of a rectangular jewelry box.

2. Be a performer on your "TV." Do a funny newscast. Learn the words of a song and "lip-synch" (moving your lips as if you were singing) while you play it.

3. Write a script for a radio or TV show. You can create your own version of a favorite book, a fairy tale, or myth. Or you might want to invent characters and a story. It's fun to get family or friends to join in on reading the script. You could actually perform it on a tape recorder or video recorder.

4. What were your grandparents' and parents' favorite radio and TV shows when they were children? How much were they allowed to watch or listen?

**Recording today:**
What are your favorite radio or television shows? What do you like about them? Write about them here.

**Imagining tomorrow:**
What do you imagine radio and TV will be like in the future? What kind of shows would be fun to have? Make up a TV or radio guide for the twenty-first century.

*Extra! Extra! Read all about it!* Newspaper boys used to call this out to people
passing in the the street. They were trying to get customers to buy their paper
and read all the latest news.

We rely on *the press* to inform us
about what's happening in the world.
That means newspapers, magazines,
and TV and radio news. But journal-
ism—telling the news in one of
these forms—doesn't go back far in
history.

In the past, people had other ways
of getting news. Early Romans could
read a news sheet that was hung up
in the street. Government officials in
ancient China could read a published
news report called a *pao*. Some merchants in the Middle Ages put out handwritten newsletters. In Europe and early
America, town criers reported news by
shouting it out on the street. People
could buy printed ballads that told
a story of what was going on, or
*broadsides*, large sheets of paper
printed on one side. All of these gave
just one story at a time. Newspapers,
which started in the 1600s, were different because they reported more
than one event.

Today's newspapers have a lot of
sections. There's news of the world,
country, state, and community. "Fea-
tures" tell stories of human interest. There are articles on sports, science, cooking, books, the arts,
leisure activities, business, home improvement,
gardening, games, and much more. Editorials explain the paper's stand on public issues. Colum-
nists write about their opinions on almost anything. There are fun things, like puzzles and—of
course—the comics. Advertising usually takes up
a lot of space. It's one of the ways the paper gets
money to publish. Advertising offers a service to
shoppers, too. Tabloid newspapers have smaller
pages and usually are devoted more to gossip than
real news. That's where you see headlines like "Elvis
Kidnapped by UFOs!"

Magazines, like newspapers, started only after
the printing press made copying easy. They contain a variety of articles, stories, and poems, often
with pictures. Some are devoted to a particular interest, like hobbies, arts, science, literature, sports,
or business. Others are meant for one group of
people. There are magazines for children, teenag-
ers, parents, and older people. Some magazines
appeal to people in a specific job. News magazines,
gossip magazines, you name it! There is probably
a magazine for every interest that people have.

The First Amendment to the U.S. Constitution guarantees "the freedom of the press." In a
democracy, that freedom is very important. It
means that a government can't control the news
to make us think in a particular way. With a free
press, we can make up our own minds about what
we believe.

## Activities:

1. Appoint a family "town crier" to spread the word about mealtime, family achievements, family plans, and other family news to everyone in your house.

2. Create your own special magazine. Write or find articles of interest to you, and illustrate with pictures you like.

3. Start a neighborhood or a family newspaper. Put in news about birthdays, vacations, visitors, new pets, people going to camp, etc. Give it a snazzy name! Ask people for news. Write articles that answer the five W's: who, what, when, where, why? Make headlines. The paper could be hand-printed or produced on a computer or typewriter.

4. Make a collage of pictures cut from magazines to hang up in your room.

5. Create a zany publication by cutting up different newspaper or magazine articles and combining the parts to make silly stories. Mismatch headlines and photographs to make the new story even wilder.

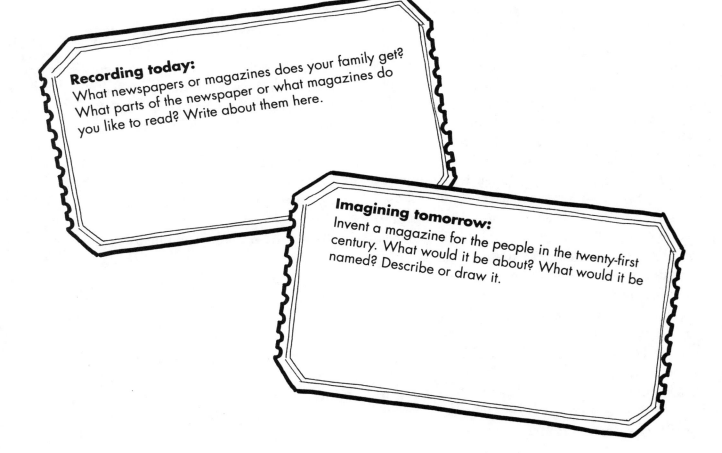

**Recording today:**
What newspapers or magazines does your family get? What parts of the newspaper or what magazines do you like to read? Write about them here.

**Imagining tomorrow:**
Invent a magazine for the people in the twenty-first century. What would it be about? What would it be named? Describe or draw it.

# Cruising the Information Superhighway

Do you *surf the Net?* Do you have a *Web page?* Are you riding on the *Information Superhighway?* Phrases nobody had heard just a few years ago are common today. Next year we'll all know new words to describe what we can do with a computer.

For most of human history, to "compute" meant to count or figure numbers. It's hard to remember numbers and do arithmetic just in your head. We've always tried to find something that will help us compute. The first people moved stones or made notches on sticks. Later, we learned to mark numbers on clay tablets, animal skins, and then paper. When someone invented the abacus, humans had a fast and accurate way to calculate numbers. For centuries, the abacus was our best computing tool. Then, in the middle 1800s, an Englishman named Charles Babbage invented a mechanical adding machine. That gave banks and businesses a way to be more accurate.

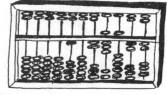

In 1935, an American, John Atanasoff, invented a computer that could run on electricity. But the first full-scale real computer didn't appear until 1945. Its name was ENIAC. This computer amazed the world. It was two stories high and took up fifteen thousand square feet of space. It weighed thirty tons and cost more than $45 million. Today, your little hand-held calculator has more power and can do more things than ENIAC!

The *integrated circuit* invented by Robert N. Noyce in 1957 replaced ENIAC's miles and miles of wires and other components. By the 1960s, many businesses were using computers. They still weren't like the ones you know, though. Then in 1971, the *microprocessor chip* changed everything. Chips are "mighty mites," tiny but efficient. Now we have much smaller computers. The first personal computers appeared in 1974. Today, there are thousands of different kinds of computers, and we use them just about everywhere.

So the "Information Superhighway" was born. Computers are not just for calculating numbers anymore. They've become a major tool for getting information. They have also become a way for people to communicate with each other. Computers can be linked to each other through telephone lines. The Internet is one such network. It's like a big bulletin board, post office, telephone, and printing press all in one. People can send and receive information of all kinds. They can do it even more easily if they're on the World Wide Web.

Today's computers can copy and change photographs, play CDs, create art, and do much more. Almost every month sees improvements in the computer. By the time you read this chapter, new developments will have already made some of it outdated. The computer has made changes in our society that are as revolutionary as the invention of the wheel or machines. One word of caution, though: anybody can put any information out on the Information Superhighway. Don't believe everything you see there just because it's on the computer!

## Activities:

1. Find out how you can use your library's computer to find books.

2. Learn to use an abacus and see how fast you can compute on it.

3. Find out how to use whatever computer is available to you. What can you do on it?

4. Make a skit or puppet show about somebody who has trouble using a computer.

**Recording today:**
Do you use a computer at school or at home? Write about it here.

**Imagining tomorrow:**
What do you think we might be using computers to do for us in the twenty-first century? Draw or write about some future computers.

# Bibliography

Amsbary, George S., managing ed. *Childcraft.* Chicago: Field Enterprises Educational Corporation, 1964.

Bennett, Steve, and Ruth Bennett. *Cabin Fever.* New York: Penguin Books, 1994.

———. *365 Outdoor Activities.* Holbrook, MA: Bob Adams, 1993.

Bowen, Ezra, series ed. *This Fabulous Century.* New York: Time-Life Books, 1970.

Cassell, Sylvia. *Indoor Games and Activities.* New York: Harper and Brothers, 1960.

Kalman, Bobbie, and David Schimpky. *Old-Time Toys.* New York: Crabtree Publishing Company, 1995.

Krueger, Caryl W. *1,001 Things to Do with Your Kids.* Nashville, TN: Abingdon Press, 1988.

Lomax, Alan, *The Folk Songs of North America.* Garden City, NY: Doubleday & Company, 1960.

Lomax, John, and Alan Lomax, *Folk Song U.S.A.* New York: Duell, Sloan and Pearce, 1962.

Lynes, Russell. *The Domesticated Americans.* New York: Harper & Row, 1963.

Matthews, Rupert, et al. *2,500 Fascinating Facts.* New York: Barnes and Noble Books, 1995.

McHenry, Robert, ed. in chief. *The New Encyclopedia Brittanica.* Chicago: Encyclopedia Brittanica, 1994.

Montagne, Prosper. *Larousse Gastronomique.* New York: Crown Publishers, 1961.

*PC Guide Introduction to Computers.* Norcross, GA: ITC Publishing Group, 1994.

Pool, Daniel. *What Jane Austen Ate and Charles Dickens Knew.* New York: Simon and Schuster, 1993.

Rowland-Entwistle, Theodore, and Jean Cooke. *The World Almanac Infopedia.* New York: World Almanac, 1990.

*The World Book Encyclopedia.* Chicago: Field Enterprises Educational Corporation, 1975.

# Index of Topics and Activities

# Index of Terms and Names

**Etcetera**

# Etcetera

**Etcetera**

# Etcetera

**Etcetera**